101 Travel Bits: The Florida Keys and Overseas Highway

The Travel Bits™ Series
A division of Tchop Street LLC

Table of Contents

Introduction

Travel Bits are not your typical guidebooks. In fact, they are not guidebooks at all!

Each collection of Travel Bits consists of 101 "bits" of information about one of the great places to visit in the world. This could be a "bit" of history, a "bit" of information on a tourist attraction, or a "bit" of something else interesting about the location.

A Travel Bits collection is not intended to be a guidebook to any particular location. You will not find the maps or pictures you would expect in a guidebook in any Travel Bits collection. Each collection gives you information a typical guidebook ignores or, when it does address the topic, only gives you a basic amount of information. This is the history, the fun facts, and the interesting sights along the way that those of us at Travel Bits find to be one of the best parts of travel.

This is not to say that there are no pictures involved in a Travel Bits collection. Each Travel Bits collection is optimized for reading as an e-book. This format makes each Travel Bit interactive, with links to official websites, maps, and pictures where it is appropriate. Thus, instead of raising the cost of the book to include pictures, we take advantage of the Internet's enormous wealth of information to take you to where the pictures already exist.

In case it is not obvious, because of the interactive nature of e-books, we highly recommend reading the Travel Bits collections using an e-book reader, as the print versions do not have these interactive features. However, the print versions of the books still have the same great content that is found in the e-book versions.

We welcome your comments. Please go to the Travel Bits website, www.101travelbits.com, for information on how to let us know your thoughts.

If you are so inclined, we would love it if you would leave an online review or reviews wherever you purchased this book and let others know how much you enjoyed it.

A Note from the Founder

If you have previously read one of the books in the 101 Travel Bits series, you know I typically use this space to discuss my relationship to the place I am writing about. Sometimes, this is a funny story about the place, and other times, it is a memory from some past road trip. However, this year, I'm doing something different.

As everyone knows, things in 2020 were not quite as anyone expected them to be. With COVID-19, travel became a much different prospect than it had been in the past. Some of the locations in the 101 Travel Bits series, like the Alaska Highway, which travels through Canada, became almost impossible for Americans to visit. Other locations, like the national parks, remained popular travel destinations. To everyone who purchased our books during 2020, thank you — as someone who loves to travel, it makes me happy to see that others, whether traveling or not, were at least thinking about hitting the road when this is over, if not before.

COVID-19 has brought about some changes to how we do things at 101 Travel Bits. Every year, we update each of the books in the 101 Travel Bits series to reflect changes that happened over the course of the previous year to the locations featured in the books. Sometimes, these are minor changes, like revising a broken link to a website or adding some new and useful information to an entry. Other times, we entirely change an entry, such as when a location is permanently closed, and we replace it with something entirely new.

This year, we could change almost every entry to reflect temporary changes brought about by COVID-19. However, we have chosen not to do that. Such changes are, by their nature, temporary. Moreover, many of those changes — for instance, the number of guests allowed to visit an attraction — may change depending on orders that are updated more often than our books.

Thus, the changes we have made to the books in the updated 2021 versions are the typical changes we make every year. Because we have not changed any entries to reflect temporary COVID-19 changes, we highly encourage you to visit any appropriate websites or call locations you may be visiting to learn what regulations may be in place or if a site is currently open.

Hopefully when we do the 2022 updates to the 101 Travel Bits series, I'll be writing to you about family road trips and funny stories about places in the books. Until then, though, at least we can plan that next trip, even if we can't take it in quite the normal way.

As always, thank you for reading!

Sarah Ferguson

Travel Bit Number 1: The Florida Keys

From Florida's Biscayne Bay to the Dry Tortugas, a series of small islands known today as the Florida Keys stretch across approximately 180 miles (290 km) of ocean in a roughly southwest direction. Lying between the Florida Straits in the Atlantic Ocean and Florida Bay in the Gulf of Mexico, the 1,700 small islands that make up the Florida Keys were exposed when ocean levels fell thousands of years ago. Most of the islands that make up the Florida Keys are extremely small; even the largest of them has no location more than four miles (6 km) from the ocean. The entirety of the land which makes up these 1,700 islands consists of only 137.3 square miles (221 km). For comparison purposes, this makes the total land area in the Florida Keys approximately the same size as the city of Las Vegas.

Today, the Florida Keys are a tourist destination for tens of thousands of tourists each year. The weather in the Keys is nearly perfect; it is the only place on the mainland of the United States that has never had a frost. The coldest temperature ever recorded in Key West, the largest city in the Florida Keys, was 41° Fahrenheit (5° C). The highest temperature ever recorded in Key West was 97° Fahrenheit (36° C). This swing of 56 degrees is less than what many parts of the United States regularly experience over the course of a single day.

Until the 1910s, the Florida Keys were only accessible by boat. This changed in 1912 with the completion of the Florida East Coast Railway extension to Key West. (Travel Bit Number 7.) This railroad from Key Largo to Key West allowed tourists and residents alike access to and from the Keys. In 1928, the Overseas Highway opened the Keys to highway travel, though this original road was not continuous; 41 miles (66 km) of the "road" consisted of water traversed by ferries.

Today, the railroad has disappeared, but the Overseas Highway now connects the mainland of the United States to Key West in an unbroken chain of road and dozens of bridges over 113 miles (182 km). (Travel Bit Number 29.)

Travel Bit Number 2: The History of the Overseas Highway

The concept for what is known today as the Overseas Highway began in 1921. At that time, the Overseas Railway provided transportation to and from the Keys, but no road connected the mainland to the fishing areas and undeveloped islands of the Keys. In an era of ever-increasing reliance on automobiles, the strict schedules and stops of the railroad were not appealing to many of the visitors and residents of the islands.

With mounting pressure to build a highway, residents of the Keys voted a bond in 1922 to provide funds to begin building what would become the Overseas Highway. Throughout the 1920s — and after the floating of a second, much larger bond to finish its construction in 1926 — construction continued. On January 25, 1928, the road from the mainland to Key West officially opened as State Road 4A.

At its opening, however, the Overseas Highway was "overseas" in more than one sense of the word. Instead of consisting of an unbroken road between the mainland and Key West, the road consisted of two long segments. The first segment was about 45 miles (70 km) from the mainland to Lower Matecumbe Key. The second segment of about 35 miles (55 km) traveled from No Name Key to Key West. In between, drivers faced a ferry ride of 41 miles (65 km) in between Lower Matecumbe Key and No Name Key. Although the ferry ride was shortened in 1931 with a lengthening of the highway, it was still inadequate to serve the needs of the road.

On Labor Day in 1935, however, the fates of the Overseas Railway and the Overseas Highway changed dramatically. On that day, one of the largest hurricanes to ever hit the United States came ashore and devastated the Upper Keys. (Travel Bit Number 41.) Among its casualties was the

Overseas Railway, which had already been in financial trouble when the hurricane struck. It did not have the financial means to rebuild the bridges along its route that the hurricane destroyed. The State of Florida stepped in and purchased the bridges and right-of-way from the railroad; this became the foundation for the completion of the full length of the Overseas Highway. The former railroad bridges — including Seven Mile Bridge, the longest bridge along the length of the Highway — were converted to handle vehicular traffic. On March 29, 1938, the Overseas Highway opened as U.S. Highway 1, which it remains today.

Travel Bit Number 3: U.S. Route 1

While nicknamed the Overseas Highway, the proper designation for the road is U.S. Route 1, or U.S. 1. Traveling in a generally north-south direction along the east coast of the United States, U.S. 1 is the longest north-south road in the United States. U.S. 1 begins at 490 Whitehead Street in Key West (Travel Bit Number 101) and ends in Fort Kent, Maine on the U.S.-Canada border 2,369 miles (3,813 km) later.

On the road from Key West to Fort Kent, U.S. 1 travels through 14 states (Florida, Georgia, South Carolina, North Carolina, Virginia, Maryland, Pennsylvania, New Jersey, New York, Connecticut, Rhode Island, Massachusetts, New Hampshire and Maine) and the District of Columbia. Among the cities it visits are Miami, Washington, D.C., Philadelphia, New York City, and Boston. U.S. 1 roughly parallels I-95, which replaced it in the 1970s as the main north-south artery connecting the states and cities of the East Coast.

Travel Bit Number 4: Card Sound Road

Travelers headed to the Overseas Highway face a choice when leaving Florida City and the mainland behind. The main road — U.S. 1 — beckons as the fastest route to Key Largo and points beyond. Alternatively, travelers can also make a left turn as they leave the mainland and head toward northern Key Largo, via Card Sound Road. The former is the main way to get to the Keys, but the latter takes visitors to a wilder part of the Keys that gives a better impression of what they looked like before the arrival of modern civilization.

The route followed by U.S. 1 today is roughly equivalent to that followed by the Overseas Railway. When the Overseas Highway was constructed during the 1920s, the route chosen followed what is now Card Sound Road. The original wooden bridge on Card Sound Road between the mainland and Key Largo remained the route for vehicular traffic to the Keys until World War II, During the war, the demands of the large military presence in the Keys required a larger bridge.

With the War bringing a larger bridge to the Keys — and a re-route of U.S. 1 from Card Sound Road to its current location — there was no need for Card Sound Road. In 1944, an uncontrolled campfire burned most of the original wooden bridge to the ground. Brave souls could still cross the bridge until 1947. That year it was permanently demolished.

With the destruction of the Card Sound Road Bridge, the community that had formed where the bridge formerly stood faced an odd situation. Located between the mainland and Key Largo, it was neither Key Largo nor the mainland. For instance, it had a Key Largo ZIP code, but mainland phone numbers. Moreover, many, if not most, of those who lived in the Card Sound community were squatting on the land and thus not legal residents of either Key Largo or the mainland.

In 1969, the potential development of the northernmost Keys as the community of Islandia (Travel Bit Number 14) led to the reconstruction of the Card Sound Bridge and the ability of residents of Card Sound to easily travel between the Keys and the mainland once again. With the reconstruction of the Card Sound Road Bridge, residents and tourists gained a second way to access the Keys. As a bonus, the reconstructed bridge created a second outlet back to the mainland in the event of a hurricane evacuation.

However, this reconstruction put the residents of the Card Sound community who were squatting on the land in a precarious legal position. Between 1975 and 2010, most of these squatters were kicked off of the land where they had been illegally residing, though often only after protracted legal battles.

Today, for a small toll, one can access the Keys via Card Sound Road. The route to the Keys via Card Sound Road is slightly longer than that via U.S. 1, but it meanders through some of the most undisturbed parts of the Keys and what little remains of the Card Sound community, providing one with a view of what the Keys were like in the not-so-distant past.

Travel Bit Number 5: Key Largo

The first of the Keys reached by travelers on the Overseas Highway is Key Largo, known as the "Diving Capital of the World" for the world-class SCUBA diving found just off its shores. Travelers using Card Sound Road arrive approximately 14 miles (23 km) as the crow flies further north on the island of Key Largo than those arriving on U.S. 1.

At approximately 30 miles (48 km) long, Key Largo is the largest of the Florida Keys. Although today Key Largo appears to be one long island, it was once composed of several smaller keys. The waterways and channels between these original keys were filled in during the construction of the Overseas Highway, creating the single island that now appears to exist. However, even this appearance is deceiving. Today, Key Largo is two islands, thanks to a manmade waterway connecting the gulf side of the island to the ocean side of the island constructed after the completion of the Overseas Highway. (Travel Bit Number 17.)

While Key Largo typically refers to the entire island, Key Largo also can refer to an unincorporated city on the island. Originally known as Rock Harbor, the city underwent a name change in the 1950s. This name change came not due to confusion or a desire for a more apt description of the city. Instead, this change happened because of two people you may have heard of: Humphrey Bogart and Lauren Bacall.

In 1948, the hit movie *Key Largo* premiered, starring Bogart and Bacall in their fourth and final film pairing. Although the filmmakers used only a few shots from the actual Key Largo, and neither Bogart nor Bacall was known to have set foot on the island during filming, the popularity of the film provided a boom to post-World War II tourism on the island. Looking to capitalize on that popularity, real estate promoters on the island of Key Largo circulated a petition asking to have the city of Rock Harbor renamed "Key Largo." The community listened to their pleas, and Rock Harbor became Key Largo. It may be the only city in the United States named after a movie.

Monroe County Tourist Development Council – Key Largo:
> www.fla-keys.com/key-largo/

Key Largo Chamber of Commerce:
> www.keylargochamber.org/

Travel Bit Number 6: Crocodile Lake National Wildlife Refuge

When traveling to Key Largo via Card Sound Road, your arrival on Key Largo is not greeted with tourist attractions, hotels, or restaurants, but with a virtually uninhabited forest and wetland. Much of this land is part of Crocodile Lake National Wildlife Refuge. The wildlife refuge is home to various endangered species, including the American Crocodile and the Key Largo Woodrat. The latter is a subspecies of the Florida Woodrat found only on Key Largo.

Although unpopulated today, in 1955, this land appeared destined for development. Speculators bought up 1,500 acres (600 ha) of this northern portion of Key Largo, and the entire area was slated for development. The speculators proceeded as far as dredging canals for boat access, but the project stalled, and nothing more ever came of their plans to develop the land.

The Nature Conservancy and the U.S. Fish and Wildlife Service eventually purchased the land, and in 1980, the Crocodile Lake National Wildlife Refuge opened. The Refuge is one of only three places in the United States where the American Crocodile breeds. When it opened, estimates placed the total population of American Crocodiles in the United States at several hundred. Today, thanks in large part to the effort of the Crocodile Lake National Wildlife Refuge, there are at least 2,000 American Crocodiles in the United States.

In an ironic twist, the success of the American Crocodile conservation effort at the Crocodile Lake National Wildlife Refuge owes much to the speculators who purchased the land in the 1950s. As part of their canal dredging operation, the speculators piled the dredged detritus of the canals on the banks of those same canals, intending to remove it later on in the development of the project. When the project stalled, no one removed the detritus. Today, this dredged material on the banks of the manmade canals provides an ideal habitat for American Crocodile nesting sites and has been a major factor in the breeding successes of American Crocodiles at Crocodile Lake.

U.S. Fish & Wildlife Service – Crocodile Lake National Wildlife Refuge: www.fws.gov/refuge/crocodile_lake/

Travel Bit Number 7: Flagler's Overseas Railway

The Overseas Highway that traverses the Florida Keys today would likely not exist except for one man and his railroad: Henry Flagler and the Florida East Coast Railway.

Henry Flagler made his initial fortune as one of the principals in Rockefeller, Andrews and Flagler, later known as Standard Oil. He originally came to Florida looking for a warmer climate to help the health of his first wife, but the Florida he found on that trip had little in the way of amenities. After remarrying following the death of his first wife, Flagler returned to the northeast coast of Florida on his honeymoon. On this trip, Flagler began to see the possibility of Florida and its vast beaches as a tourist destination. In 1885, Flagler began purchasing hotels and other buildings along the northeastern Florida coast. His efforts began to create the Florida we know today.

Flagler's story might have ended in northeast Florida. However, legend has it that Flagler asked the owners of the railroad between Jacksonville and St. Augustine to upgrade their infrastructure to accommodate the ever-larger crowds venturing to Florida to enjoy the year-round warm weather and Flagler-owned hotels. When the owners of the railroad refused to upgrade, Flagler bought the railroad outright and upgraded it himself.

By 1904, Flagler had built his initial railroad, the Florida East Coast Railway, from Jacksonville to Homestead, south of Miami. Having built a railroad linking northern Florida to southern Florida, his next project would be his most ambitious yet: extend the railroad from Homestead to Key West, approximately 120 miles (190 km) and an ocean away. In 1905, Flagler began work on what some were already calling "Flagler's Folly" — a railroad across the islands of the Keys to Key West.

For the next seven years, crews worked to construct the Overseas Railway. The construction project employed up to 4,000 men at once; they made $1.25 each day, with food, lodging, and medical care included as part of their benefits. Hurricanes in 1906, 1909, and 1910 caused major problems with construction, but ultimately, they only delayed the plans. On January 22, 1912, the first train traveling the entire route left Homestead for Key West.

Ultimately, the Overseas Railway cost $50 million to build, and every penny to build it came from the deep pockets of Henry Flagler. What had once been known as Flagler's Folly quickly became known as the Eighth Wonder of the World, and tourists flocked to travel the railroad that crossed an ocean.

As for Flagler, he was one of the passengers on the first train from Homestead to Key West. The party that greeted him in Key West lasted three days. Flagler, enjoying the festivities and completion of his work, supposedly greeted the gathered crowd upon the arrival of the first train by saying, "Now, I can die happy."

A year later, at the age of 83, Flagler did die after a fall in his Palm Beach home. His railroad across the ocean lived on for two more decades, until its destruction in one of the largest hurricanes in United States history. (Travel Bit Number 41.) Today, Flagler has given his name to many places in Florida. Even Key West remembers him with a statue located near the city's ferry terminal, which is just feet from the former terminus of the Overseas Railway.

Travel Bit Number 8: Dagny Johnson Key Largo Hammock Botanical State Park

After arriving on Key Largo via Card Sound Road, travelers shortly arrive at Dagny Johnson Key Largo Hammock Botanical State Park. A hammock, in this case, refers not to a rope bed slung between two trees, but to a stand of trees growing in an elevated area of a marsh or swampy area. The stand of West Indian hardwood hammock protected at Dagny Johnson is one of the largest in the United States.

Like so many other preserved areas in the Florida Keys, Dagny Johnson was originally slated for development into oceanfront condos. However, the land that is now Dagny Johnson received an 11th-hour reprieve before it could be developed.

Today, Dagny Johnson has earned the nickname of the "Land of the Little Giants." The park is home to the most National Champion trees in the United States. National Champion trees are those which are the largest tree of a species in a given country. Dagny Johnson holds as many records as it does because it is the northernmost spot most of these trees grow. In other words, these trees are found nowhere else in the United States, giving the park a large edge on its competition.

Visitors to Dagny Johnson can take one of two short hikes to see the hammocks after which the park is named, but you are highly encouraged stay on the paths. Two of the most poisonous trees found in the United States happen to find the 2,421 acres (980 ha) of the park to be an ideal habitat and are thus abundant throughout Dagny Johnson. One of these, the poisonwood, is common throughout the Keys. It produces urushiol, the same substance found in poison sumac and poison oak.

The other notable poisonous tree in Dagny Johnson is the manchineel, also known as the beach apple. The manchineel is one of the most poisonous trees in the world. Unlike most poisonous trees, where only the berries or leaves are poisonous, every part of the manchineel tree is poisonous. The poison of the tree is so potent that if you stand under a manchineel during a rainstorm, you will find your skin blistering as the raindrops collect the poison from the leaves above and drop it on your exposed skin. While this will probably not kill you, more prolonged or direct contact with the tree can cause serious injury or death. During a 1910 hurricane, a worker on the Overseas Railway strapped himself to a manchineel tree and nearly died. It took him weeks to fully recover.Ponce de Leon, the discoverer of Florida and seeker of the Fountain of Youth, died after being shot in the thigh by an arrow tipped with poison from a manchineel tree.

Florida State Parks – Dagny Johnson Key Largo Hammock Botanical State Park:

https://www.floridastateparks.org/park/Key-Largo-Hammock

Travel Bit Number 9: Mileage on the Overseas Highway

Although its formal name is United States Highway 1, the highway connecting Key Largo to Key West is better known as the Overseas Highway. United States Highway 1, or U.S. 1, is not just a road in the Keys; it travels over 2,000 miles (3,200 km) north to Fort Kent, Maine.

The mile markers along U.S. 1 provide travelers with a convenient method for determining their location on the road. Starting at Mile Marker 113 when leaving the mainland and entering Monroe County, the rectangular, green mile markers along U.S. 1 count down to Mile Marker 0 in the heart of Key West. Businesses and sights along the way inform visitors to the Keys of their location by noting at which Mile Marker they sit. Thus, travelers looking to visit Duck Key (Travel Bit Number 59) are told to find it at Mile 61. The Mile Markers are also helpful to tell how far you are from a certain location. The aforementioned Duck Key is 61 miles from Key West and 52 miles from the beginning of the Overseas Highway. If you know the Mile Markers for two locations, a little math can tell you how far it is between stops.

This system would be helpful on its own but is further aided by the method which is used to give addresses to locations along the highway. Homes and businesses along the highway have a four-, five- or six-digit address that reflects their specific location on the highway. The last two digits are a typical street number, but the first two to four digits denote the mileage of the home or business. Thus, 68269 is a location at mile 68.2 along the road, while 31020 is at mile 31.0. Even numbered addresses are on the gulf side of the highway; odd numbered addresses are on the ocean side of the road. Getting lost along the highway is thus a rather difficult task.

One caveat: do not try this method of addresses if you

are in Marathon. (Travel Bit Number 61.) While you can use this convenient method of finding an address for virtually the entirety of the Overseas Highway, the city of Marathon subscribes to its own, unrelated method of home and business numbering.

The marking of the Overseas Highway mileage did not begin with the highway; like so many other things along the road, the system has its roots in the Overseas Railway. Beginning at Jacksonville, the Florida East Coast Railway marked its tracks from Mile 0 to 522. The railroad used white, triangular concrete posts with the mileage information painted in black to mark the passing miles. Today, along the former route of the railroad in the Keys, only one of these original markers is found in its original location. Although it is not in good shape, you can find this marker at Mile 30 on Big Pine Key on the ocean side of the highway.

If you can't find the Mile 30 marker, there is a second original marker. This one is not, however, in its original location. Instead, it is at the Caribbean Club bar. (Travel Bit Number 13.) Some might suggest its current location is more convenient than its original one (or at least more fun).

Travel Bit Number 10: The 18 Mile Stretch

While Card Sound Road gives visitors to the Keys a taste of what the islands looked like before development, it is not the fastest route into the Keys. That distinction belongs to U.S. 1, which is the official route of the Overseas Highway.

Originally, U.S. 1 followed the route that is today Card Sound Road. However, this would change during World War II. The military in the Keys needed a short and fast route to their installations in Key West. The original route of the Overseas Railway provided just such a route; re-routing the highway from Card Sound Road to the site used by the railroad would save drivers eighteen miles on the road to Key Largo and beyond. On May 16, 1944, the so-called "18 Mile Stretch," named after its length, opened to traffic.

The 18 Mile Stretch crosses several bodies of water as it makes its way from the mainland to Key Largo. One of these is Lake Surprise, so named because the surveyors locating the Overseas Railway were surprised to find a lake where they found Lake Surprise. The 18 Mile Stretch also crosses the Intracoastal Waterway at Jewfish Creek. Jewfish Creek is named after the former term for the Goliath Grouper, a fish found throughout the Florida Keys.

Unsurprisingly, the Goliath Grouper is so-called because of its size. The huge fish can grow to over eight feet (2.4 m) long and weigh nearly half a ton (450 kg). Although the fish were fairly common during the early-1900s, they are now critically endangered, and there has been no harvest of them in the United States in over a quarter century. Today, their population is in recovery.

Goliath Groupers are known for their curiosity and fearlessness; these qualities that make them popular with divers and snorkelers also made them easy prey for fishermen. While you can no longer fish for Goliath Groupers in the United States, a quick perusal of the Internet will turn up many videos of Goliath Groupers interacting with fishermen. More impressively, the groupers will often steal fish directly from the lines of fishermen — even when the fish they are stealing are big enough to be measured in feet rather than inches.

Travel Bit Number 11: Key Largo Railroad Depot (Mile 105.6)

Although it was the most important development in the modern history of the Florida Keys, little remains of the Overseas Railway today. At Mile 105.6, the Key Largo Railroad Depot once sat in what is now the median of the Overseas Highway. Like most of the railway, this is a building which no longer exists.

Though promoted as a way to visit the Florida Keys, the construction of the Overseas Railway had a much greater impact on life in the Florida Keys than just jump-starting the tourism industry that now thrives there. Once completed, the Overseas Railway brought the Keys — for the first time in their history — dependable mail service and supplies. With almost no natural freshwater sources on the islands, the railroad could also bring water to the Keys via tank car. This water service provided an invaluable supplement to the cisterns that otherwise supplied residents of the Keys with all of their water.

In addition to making life in the Keys easier and providing a route to the islands for tourists, the railroad provided jobs to islanders. Some of these residents would have worked at stations like the Key Largo Railroad Depot as porters and stationmasters; others would have worked at repairing the railroad or on the cars themselves.

Perhaps most importantly to the residents of the Keys in the era before plane travel, the railroad gave them a method to ship their perishable agricultural products and seafood to northern locations. A fish caught in Key West on Wednesday could be dinner in New York City on Friday night, and people across the country could now enjoy pineapples and produce from the Keys.

Travel Bit Number 12: Monroe County

Except for a tiny portion of the Keys located north of Key Largo and unreachable except via boat or helicopter, the Florida Keys lie entirely within Monroe County. It is a county that has more quirks of population and geography than probably any other county in Florida, if not the entire United States.

In terms of geographic size, Monroe County is the largest county in Florida. While this suggests the county is huge, approximately three-quarters of this geographic area is water. As for the remaining quarter of Monroe County's "land," the vast majority is not part of the Keys at all. Instead, the rest of Monroe County encompasses a large swath of the Everglades on the mainland.

Although over 87 percent of the land in Monroe County is on the mainland portion of Florida in the Everglades, that part of the county is almost entirely uninhabited. Of the over 73,000 people who live in Monroe County, approximately 60 of those citizens currently live on the mainland; the rest live in the Keys. For the 60 mainland residents of Monroe County, their county seat lies about 70 miles (110 km) across water and swampland; it is a 200 mile (320 km) trip each way by car. The latter route also requires a Monroe County resident to traverse an entirely different county on his or her way to conduct county business, making for a hugely inconvenient trip.

Monroe County Official Website:
        www.monroecounty-fl.gov

Travel Bit Number 13: The Caribbean Club (Mile 104.1)

You can find drinking establishments in abundance throughout the Florida Keys. The oldest bar in the Upper Keys also happens to be one of the more famous of those drinking establishments: the Caribbean Club.

In 1940, the Caribbean Club opened along the gulf side of the Overseas Highway. The Caribbean Club could have been just another bar along the Highway, but in the summer of 1947, two Hollywood producers showed up on Key Largo for one purpose: to write the screenplay for the movie version of a Broadway play called, appropriately for the location, *Key Largo*. Many of the businesses in the Florida Keys closed during the summer months during this era, but the owner of the Caribbean Club leased it to the two producers so they could use it as a work area while they adapted the play into a screenplay. When the film version of *Key Largo* came out in 1948, only one actual location in the Florida Keys made it into the film: the façade of the Caribbean Club, where the writers wrote the screenplay for the film. The filmmakers filmed every other location in the movie in California.

Observant viewers of the film will notice that the Caribbean Club of the movie is much larger than the present-day building and includes a hotel, which features prominently in the plot of the film. In 1955, a fire gutted the hotel portion of the Caribbean Club, which was torn down and never rebuilt.

Today, the Caribbean Club still sits along the gulf side of the Overseas Highway, indulging travelers who wish to stop for a beverage and a water view. The site is also home to one of the two original markers for the Overseas Railway remaining in the Keys. (Travel Bit Number 7.) This marker is not in its original location; the original location was approximately two miles (3 km) further north of the

Caribbean Club.

Travel Bit Number 14: Islandia

On December 6, 1960, the community of Islandia was incorporated as a Dade County municipality when thirteen of its eighteen registered voters approved incorporation. Islandia, consisting of the 33 northernmost Keys, included 13 major islands and was a most Floridian of real estate schemes: for the next 30 years, Islandia's municipal government existed as a ruse. None of the voters who chose the government lived in Islandia. Instead, they served as absentee landowners who voted themselves into power from Miami real estate offices.

At its outset, its investors envisioned Islandia as a legitimate real estate and resort development. As soon as it was incorporated, however, Islandia faced extreme opposition from environmentalists, who wished to preserve these undeveloped Keys. With a great deal of interest in the project from both investors and environmentalists, the federal government stepped in and started buying up land in Islandia when it came available. Eventually, the federal government used the land it was buying to create Biscayne National Monument, and later, Biscayne National Park. The few actual residents of Islandia objected to this federal purchasing of land, viewing it as an obstruction of development that could make them rich. To protest, they cleared a 125 foot (38 m) swath down the middle of one of the islands.

Ultimately, the only part of Islandia to be developed was the reconstruction of Card Sound Bridge. (Travel Bit Number 4.) Though its investors never developed it, you can still visit the aforementioned swath cut through Elliott Island, either in person or via satellite views. It is now a nature trail known to some as "Spite Highway."

As for the community of Islandia, the scheme whereby its investors governed it from Miami was eventually discovered, though it took until 2012 for the Miami-Dade

County Commission to formally abolish Islandia as a municipality.

Travel Bit Number 15: The Key Largo Rock Castle (Mile 103.5)

In 1935, the Upper Keys were devastated by the Labor Day Hurricane, one of the largest hurricanes to ever hit the United States. (Travel Bit Number 41.) The devastation from this storm means little that existed before 1935 remains in the Upper Keys today. Key Largo is home to one of the few buildings to have survived the hurricane in this part of the islands: the Key Largo Rock Castle, also known as the Largo Sound Rock Castle.

The Key Largo Rock Castle was built during the 1920s by a New Jersey dentist. With two turrets, the Key Largo Rock Castle as originally built resembled a castle. Rather than using stone for construction material, the "rocks" from which it was constructed were pieces of quarried coral from the island itself. The walls of the Castle are, however, constructed with a castle-like thickness; they are almost three feet (1 m) thick at the bottom, tapering to sixteen inches (40 cm) at their peak.

During the Labor Day Hurricane, as the storm destroyed buildings around it, the ocean surge flooded the lower floors of the Castle. The dentist was not in the Keys during the hurricane, but his wife was. She was forced to take refuge in one of the Castle's turrets. As the water and storm surge rose, the furniture from the floors below rose with the rising water and began banging on the ceiling beneath her feet. The noise lasted throughout the night and may be the reason why many people today say that the Castle is haunted — though by whom or what remains unknown.

Travel Bit Number 16: Black Caesar

The pirates who roamed the Caribbean are infamous still today, and the Keys played host to many of them over the years. (Travel Bit Number 67.) One of the lesser known pirates who made the Keys his base of operations was a pirate known as Black Caesar.

Black Caesar began life in Africa. He was a chief who avoided capture by the slave traders for many years until slave traders enticed him onto a ship with food, drink and the promise of jewels. Once on board, the captain of the ship lifted anchor, and Black Caesar and his men found themselves outnumbered and outgunned, to be sold into slavery once the ship reached the Americas. As the slave ship approached Florida, a sailor who had befriended Black Caesar released his shackles as a hurricane tossed the slave ship. The sailor and Black Caesar abandoned ship by a small boat and were the only survivors as their ship wrecked in the winds.

Wrecked, the sailor and Black Caesar found themselves on the Keys between Miami and Key Largo. They made their home on Elliott Island and from there began careers of piracy. From the island, the two men along with others they had recruited would pose as shipwrecked sailors. Passing ships would stop to rescue men who they believed were sailors; Black Caesar and his men would then loot the ships that had sought to "rescue" them. Their home on Elliott Key eventually became a large pirate base. As for the sailor, Black Caesar eventually killed the friend who rescued him from the slave ship in an argument over a woman.

After killing his friend, Black Caesar eventually moved to ship-based piracy. He met Blackbeard, who he joined in terrorizing Mid-Atlantic shipping as a lieutenant aboard the Queen Anne's Revenge. In 1718, when Blackbeard was killed, Black Caesar was captured during the fight and hung at

Williamsburg, Virginia.

Travel Bit Number 17: The Cut (Mile 103.4)

One of the shortest bridges on the Overseas Highway crosses a location most call "The Cut" but which is officially known as "The Marvin D. Adams Waterway." The Cut (as we shall refer to it) is a manmade waterway that cuts the island of Key Largo in two, hence its nickname. The manmade nature is unmistakable when passing over the waterway: the walls of the waterway stretch straight and tall, several feet above sea level and the water.

The Cut was the brainchild of an insurance salesman/real estate investor named Marvin D. Adams. In the early 1950s, Mr. Adams purchased 50 acres (20 ha) of land in Key Largo. At the time, those who wished to travel from the gulf side of Key Largo to the ocean side of Key Largo via boat had a problem—at 33 miles (53 km) long, it was a long way, particularly on a slow boat. This length was not a bad thing for people looking for a relaxing boat journey. However, it was a major problem for small boats caught in a storm on the ocean side who needed to return to the relative safety of the gulf side. It was also annoying to those who were impatient and looking to get to the other side of the island quickly.

The land Mr. Adams purchased happened to stretch across Key Largo at its narrowest point, and Mr. Adams had a plan: he would cut a canal through the center of the island. The fill from The Cut would be valuable, but there was even more profit in the increased value of his land. The formerly landlocked land would now be waterfront property and have easy access to both the gulf and the ocean for those looking to purchase it from him. Mr. Adams began to cut his canal across Key Largo in the late 1950s; it opened in early 1961, splitting Key Largo into two islands and creating the only manmade path to cross between the gulf and the ocean in all of the Florida Keys.

Travel Bit Number 18: The Florida Reef

While many — if not most — visitors to the Florida Keys will remain on dry land for their visit, the most important geologic feature of the Florida Keys is approximately four to seven miles (6 to 11 km) off the coast of the islands: the Florida Reef.

Also known as the Great Florida Reef, the Florida Reef Tract and the Florida Key Reef, the Florida Reef is the third largest coral barrier reef in the world, after only the Great Barrier Reef in Australia and the Belize Barrier Reef off the coast of Belize. The Florida Reef extends from the coastal waters near Miami to just south of the Marquesas Keys, about 20 miles (30 km) west of Key West. Although often referred to as a single reef, the Florida Reef consists of approximately 6,000 individual reefs that are from 5,000 to 7,000 years old. Divers on the reef can find over 40 species of stony corals (Travel Bit Number 37) and over 500 species of fish; in total, there are over 1,400 species of plants and animals who call the Florida Reef home. Divers spend millions of dollars every year just to get an up-close view of the only living coral reef in the continental United States.

While the Florida Reef would attract huge numbers for its beauty alone, divers on the Reef have a second compelling reason to visit: it is the location of hundreds of shipwrecks. The Florida Reef hugs the Gulf Stream, which has been one of the main shipping channels through the Caribbean since Europeans arrived in North America. Before modern navigational equipment and lighthouses, the Florida Reef was a major hazard for ships — if they strayed from the Gulf Stream due to navigational error or a storm, they could easily find themselves wrecked on the reef.

The number of shipwrecks on the reef reached its height during the mid-19th century. During this period, approximately one ship per week wrecked on the Florida Reef, and an entire industry of salvaging wrecked ships grew up around the shipwrecks. (Travel Bit Number 25.) Many of the individual reefs that make up the Florida Reef are named after shipwrecks from this period, and divers can spend a lifetime visiting these shipwrecks—or searching for ships known to have wrecked on the reef but whose final resting places remain unknown.

Travel Bit Number 19: John Pennekamp Coral Reef State Park (Mile 102.5)

Key Largo is home to the first underwater state park in the United States: John Pennekamp Coral Reef State Park. Established in 1963, the State Park extends three miles (5 km) into the Atlantic Ocean and is twenty-five miles (40 km) long. Together with the Florida Keys National Marine Sanctuary, these two preserves protect over 178 square nautical miles (286 km) of reefs, seagrass beds, and mangrove swamps throughout the Keys.

Although it stretches over a hundred miles (160 km), perhaps the prettiest portion of the Florida Reef is that encompassed by John Pennekamp Coral Reef State Park. Key Largo's length protects the reef from the waters of Florida Bay; further out in the Keys, this water flows on to the reefs and limits the growth of the corals that make it such a spectacular diving destination.

Until the 1950s, no one saw the reef as a commodity for tourism. Until then, the reef was valuable in that it provided large amounts of coral and conch that tourists could purchase; portions of the reef were even dynamited to obtain the coral quickly. In the 1950s, conservationist Dr. Gilbert L. Voss and John Pennekamp (a newspaper editor who was instrumental in preserving the Everglades in the previous decades) recognized the need to preserve the Florida Reef and began seeking to preserve it as an underwater sanctuary. In 1963, their efforts — and a private donation of land for the park's land-based entrance that was, at the time, the most valuable donation ever made to a state park anywhere in the United States — led to the opening of John Pennekamp Coral Reef State Park.

Today, the State Park continues to work to preserve the reef and provide visitors to the Keys information on that which lies under the water. SCUBA divers and snorkelers flock to see the reef, shipwrecks, and the famous "Christ of the Deep" statue that lie in its waters. Those who are less inclined to diving can look at the reef on a glass bottom boat trip or visit the park's Visitor Center and view informational exhibits and a 30,000-gallon aquarium.

Florida State Parks – John Pennekamp Coral Reef State Park: www.floridastateparks.org/park/Pennekamp

Travel Bit Number 20: The Spiegel Grove

For thousands of years, people have created artificial reefs. Ancient people created reefs for protection of shipping and warfare, while today's artificial reefs protect shorelines and create habitats for ocean creatures. The Florida Keys are home to one of the more famous of these artificial reefs: the Spiegel Grove.

Commissioned in 1956, the U.S.S. Spiegel Grove was a 510 foot (155 m) long landing ship, with a complement of eighteen officers and 300 crew. During her active service, she spent most of her time in amphibious exercises along the eastern seaboard and the Caribbean. She was decommissioned in 1989 and transferred to the "mothball" fleet in the James River. In 1998, title on the Spiegel Grove passed to the State of Florida, which intended to sink the Spiegel Grove in waters off of Key Largo to form an artificial reef. The state intended to make the Spiegel Grove the largest purposely-scuttled ship used to establish a reef community up to that point in time.

On May 2, 2002, after nearly a year of cleaning and preparation for its sinking, the Spiegel Grove was moved from Virginia to Florida. As crews made final preparations for her sinking, the Spiegel Grove rolled to her starboard side, requiring the workers preparing her for sinking to abandon ship. Although no one was hurt, the Spiegel Grove ended up sinking earlier than planned, and she settled upside-down on the ocean floor with her bow out of the water. A month later, crews rolled the ship from her upside-down position to her starboard side; although the original plan had been to sink her upright, the problems with the premature sinking forced a change in the original plan.

Three years after her sinking, Hurricane Dennis passed through the Florida Keys. After the storm had passed, divers found a major impact of the Hurricane off of Key Largo: the

Spiegel Grove, which had been lying on her starboard side, was now upright—the position in which she was intended to be sunk before the accident shifted those plans.

Over a decade later, the Spiegel Grove remains both upright and a popular dive site. She attracts a large amount of marine life and is larger than any natural underwater feature in the Keys. With her long length, some people claim that divers can dive the wreck a hundred times and still not see the whole ship.

Travel Bit Number 21: Key Largo Lighthouse (Mile 99.4)

During the 1800s, work to erect lighthouses and thus protect shipping along the dangerous waters of the Florida Reef commenced. (Travel Bit Number 69.) One of those lighthouses was erected at Rebecca Shoal, a portion of coral reef about 25 miles (40 km) west of Key West. The reef at Rebecca Shoal is only eleven feet underwater and surrounded by much deeper and passable waters. The need for a lighthouse on the shoal was thus obvious and imperative. Rebecca Shoal is also subject to strong currents and rough seas, and erecting a lighthouse there proved extremely difficult. After three decades of attempts, the lighthouse at Rebecca Shoal finally commenced operation in 1886.

For approximately 40 years, keepers manned the Rebecca Shoal Lighthouse. During poor weather, supplying the lighthouse was nearly impossible. Even in good weather, the lighthouse was beyond easy reach. In 1902, perhaps because of the harsh conditions at the lighthouse, one of the three lighthouse keepers went mad and fell—or jumped, depending on who is telling the story—to his death. In 1919, a major hurricane blew across Rebecca Shoal. The hurricane shattered the glass of the lighthouse and damaged its lens; just a few miles east of the lighthouse, a Spanish steamer perished in the storm's winds, with all 488 people aboard losing their lives.

In 1926, the Rebecca Shoal lighthouse was automated, negating the need for a lighthouse keeper at the dangerous post. Many of the older parts of the lighthouse were scrapped in 1953. In 1959, a Key Largo homeowner looking to build a non-functioning—but attractive—lighthouse on his property found himself in north-central Florida, purchasing a traditional lighthouse lantern from a scrapyard. He had no idea where the lantern had come from, but the look was what he coveted for his own (fake) lighthouse.

Fast forward 40 years, and the fake Key Largo lighthouse was in disrepair. Rather than destroy the building, a new homeowner decided to repair it. As part of the process, he looked into the provenance of the lantern. What he discovered shocked him. The new homeowner had a major piece of Florida Keys history sitting in his backyard: the lantern in his fake lighthouse was the original lantern from the old Rebecca Shoal Lighthouse. Today, the lantern, which is all that remains of the original Rebecca Shoal Lighthouse, has been restored as part of the fake Key Largo lighthouse. It now serves its owners as a private guest home with an unusual history.

Travel Bit Number 22: The Discovery and Long, Uninhabited History of the Florida Keys

On May 15, 1513, Ponce de Léon became the first European to see the Florida Keys. He called them "Los Martires." As noted by the chronicler of the voyage, the islands were so-called "because seen from a distance, the rocks as they rose to view appeared like men who were suffering. The name remained fitting because of the many who have been lost there since." Despite naming them, it is unlikely anyone from Ponce de Léon's initial voyage of discovery even stepped foot on any of the Keys.

In 1733, a Spanish fleet — *flota* in Spanish — wrecked in the Keys as they fled a hurricane. Today, the wrecks of those ships are found along 80 miles (130 km) of the coastline of the Upper and Middle Keys. Thanks to this disaster, the Spanish drafted the first known map of the Keys, hoping (in vain) to prevent future shipwrecks. Beyond their location on a map, the Spanish were uninterested in the Florida Keys because they were devoid of gold and silver. Thus, while Europeans settled the rest of the Caribbean, the Keys remained uninhabited.

It took until the 1800s, when Spain ceded Florida to the United States, that any significant habitation in the Keys took place. In 1822, the first permanent establishment in the Keys — Key West — took hold. From that point forward, the Keys gradually became the inhabited islands that they are today.

Travel Bit Number 23: The Natural History of the Keys

Geographically speaking, the Florida Keys are an island archipelago lying along the Florida Straits. The Keys mark the division between the Gulf of Mexico and the Atlantic Ocean. The islands that make up the Florida Keys are, for the most part, what remains of a coral reef that is now above water. In the past, sea levels were higher and with now-lower water levels, these former reefs are islands. Not all of the islands are former reefs, though. Some of the Keys are mud islands in Florida Bay (the gulf side of the Keys) and others are sandy islands (like the Dry Tortugas).

In addition to marking the boundary between the Gulf of Mexico and the Atlantic Ocean, the Florida Keys form one of the strongest cultural boundaries in the Americas. Historically, the islands marked a boundary between agricultural systems. In Florida, the native peoples grew seed crops from Mexico; in the Bahamas and Caribbean, the natives grew root crops from South America.

Today, the Florida Keys seem like a natural paradise, but people have altered most of the inhabited islands from their natural states. There are dredged canals, landfill that increased the islands' natural shoreline, and many changes to flora and fauna brought about by the settlement of the islands. Just looking at a satellite image of the Keys, some of these changes are obvious, particularly the straight canals cut into the islands. Although these changes may last forever, many efforts are being made to preserve the remaining natural habitats, flora, and fauna of the Keys so that generations to come will be able to enjoy at least some parts of the islands in their natural form.

Travel Bit Number 24: The African Queen (Mile 99.7)

Although the movie *Key Largo* was not filmed in the Keys, enterprising individuals in the Keys have taken advantage of the film since its release, going so far as to rename an entire city to capitalize on its fame. (Travel Bit Number 26.) Although not quite as drastic as changing a city's name, *Key Largo* is the reason a movie prop from an African film is now resting next to a chain hotel on Key Largo. It is there on Key Largo, next to the Holiday Inn, where the steamboat from the movie *The African Queen* sits.

The connection between *The African Queen* and the Florida Keys is tangential. Humphrey Bogart, star of *Key Largo*, also starred in *The African Queen*. This minor connection was enough to convince someone to bring the boat from Africa to Key Largo. Beyond this most fleeting of connections, there is no reason to find the steamboat from *The African Queen* on Key Largo. Except, maybe, this connection. Bogart, a hard drinker, might have loved the Keys, which many view as a drinking man's paradise. During the filming of *The African Queen*, Bogart bragged that he was the only one on location in Africa who did not get sick. The reason? He never drank the African water, as he preferred to drink the ample supply of whiskey he had brought with him from the United States.

Travel Bit Number 25: Wrecking & Wreckers

From the time of the first Spanish wrecks upon the islands of the Florida Keys until the lighthouses that line the islands were finished in the late 1800s, the major industry in the Florida Keys was the wrecking industry. "Wrecking" is the process of salvaging shipwrecks—a ship would wreck upon the reefs and rocks around the Keys, and wreckers (the people who worked at wrecking) would salvage the ship and its goods for financial remuneration.

During the mid-1800s, ships wrecked in the Keys at a rate of nearly one per week. The process of wrecking: the wreckers would see or hear of a shipwreck and arrive at its location. The first to arrive was the wreck master and would be responsible for the wrecking process. Wreckers were first obligated to save passengers and crew. Once that process finished, the wreckers would salvage as much cargo as possible. Sometimes an entire ship itself could be recovered. The process of off-loading goods could lighten the ship enough so that it would re-float and get off of whatever shoal or rock upon which it had wrecked.

Once the wreckers salvaged everything they could from a wreck, they would take the salvaged goods to Key West. At the federal court in Key West, the salvaged goods would be appraised and auctioned off. The proceeds were then distributed to the wreckers in fixed percentages depending on their role in the wrecking process. At the height of the wrecking industry, the court would have hundreds of cases on its books at any given time.

Although the process for dealing with a wreck was orderly and ordained, many stories of misbehavior from the wreckers have been passed down. Before the federal court established the orderly process, the original wreckers would not only plunder the ships that wrecked but kill or capture anyone who survived them. When the process for wrecking became settled, this still did not solve all the problems. Once the wreckers completed salvaging a ship, they would set a ship on fire. The fire would destroy the ship, and others passing the area could not see the remains of the ship. There would, therefore, be a greater potential for another wreck at the same location. Once the government began to construct lighthouses, wreckers would supposedly extinguish the lighthouse beacons or light additional beacons elsewhere in the hopes of confusing a ship captain and driving him on to a hazard.

With the construction of the lighthouses in the Keys, the wrecking industry died out as the wrecks became few and far between. The last significant shipwreck was in 1905, and the last of the local Keys wreckers was bought out in 1920.

Travel Bit Number 26: Rock Harbor (Mile 100.0)

The small community of Rock Harbor once sat along the Overseas Railway from approximately Mile Marker 100 to 95. The post office and train depot for the small community were located at approximately Mile Marker 98.5. Like other minor stops along the railroad, if no passengers were exiting or getting on the train at Rock Harbor, it didn't stop. To deliver the mail, someone tossed it off of the still-moving train as they passed the depot. Similarly, someone else on the train hooked outbound mail using a pole equipped for just that purpose.

Those traveling across Key Largo today will not find any official trace of the small community of Rock Harbor. As noted in Travel Bit Number 5, real estate speculators and others in Rock Harbor realized that the release of the film *Key Largo* provided them with an invaluable opportunity to promote their town, and they renamed it Key Largo. On May 31, 1952, letters originating at the post office came from Rock Harbor. On June 1, 1952, letters originating at the post office came from Key Largo. With this overnight name change, the real estate speculators had given their properties instant name recognition. They had also relegated Rock Harbor to its current situation as an interesting bit of Florida Keys trivia.

Despite being one of the larger communities in the Keys, Key Largo, like Rock Harbor before it, is not an officially incorporated town. There are three separate communities on Key Largo (Key Largo, North Key Largo, and Tavernier), and they are all unincorporated. There are very few incorporated cities and towns in the Keys. The only currently incorporated cities on the islands are Key West, Key Colony Beach, Marathon, Layton, and Islamorada.

Travel Bit Number 27: Hurricanes

Hurricane season in the Florida Keys runs from June 1 to November 30, though the greatest likelihood of hurricanes is from August 15 to October 1. In any given year, there is a one in seven chance of a hurricane hitting the Lower Keys.

Historically, hurricanes have been a major part of life in and near the Keys. On September 15, 1622, a hurricane struck a Spanish treasure fleet sailing out of Havana as it passed by the Keys. This hurricane sank or grounded eight of the fleet's ships and killed over 500 people. One of the ships sunk in this hurricane was the *Nuestra Señora de Atocha*. The ship sank about 35 miles (55 km) west of present-day Key West, near the Dry Tortugas. Though the ship initially sank in 55 feet (17 m) of water, she was considered salvageable. Then, on October 5, a second hurricane struck the Keys and scattered the wreck across the sea floor. This second hurricane made salvage of the ship an impossibility in 1622. Over 360 years later, the wreck of the *Atocha* would be found by Mel Fisher and salvaged using modern methods. Nearly half a billion dollars' worth of treasure has already been brought up from the wreck. Even better for those who profit from the ship, the portion of the ship where most of the valuables were stored has yet to be found. The story of the *Atocha* is detailed further in 101 Travel Bits: Key West.

In 1759, a hurricane in the Keys caused the Dry Tortugas to disappear temporarily. A decade later, Key Largo's highest trees disappeared beneath floodwaters during a hurricane. The Great Hurricane of 1846 destroyed 592 of 600 houses in Key West, demolished two lighthouses, and left Key West with water eight feet (2.5 m) deep on some streets. A 1906 hurricane killed about 160 people and destroyed much of the Overseas Railway, which was under construction at the time. In 1919, a hurricane hit Key West and sunk a Spanish steamer, killing all 488 people aboard. Hurricane Donna in 1960 destroyed the Tea Table Key Relief Channel Bridge and temporarily isolated most of the Keys. In 2017, Hurricane Irma in 2017 destroyed almost 1,200 homes and affected approximately 36,000 other homes. Ultimately, only 13 percent of the homes in the Keys were unaffected by the storm.

While the ability to predict hurricanes has improved dramatically since the days of the Spanish treasure fleets, they remain a danger for much of the year in the Keys. With only one road in and out of the islands, it is a difficult place to evacuate; one reason for the Card Sound Bridge reconstruction was to have a second way off of the islands in the event of a hurricane. Unfortunately, it has proved valuable during hurricanes in the past and will likely prove valuable in the future.

Travel Bit Number 28: Florida Keys Wild Bird Rehabilitation Center (Mile 93.6)

One of the many institutions in the Florida Keys that helps rehabilitate wild animals is the Florida Keys Wild Bird Rehabilitation Center. Laura Quinn, a statistician and math teacher who relocated to the Florida Keys with her husband, founded the center. A bird lover, Quinn started rehabilitating wild birds in her backyard with the help of a local veterinarian.

Eventually, Quinn's rehabilitation project outgrew the backyard, and she obtained a small amount of acreage where she could rehabilitate the native birds of the Keys. In 1991, the Florida Keys Wild Bird Center opened, with the purpose of rehabilitating those birds it could and rehoming those who were too injured to be released back into the wild. Although Quinn passed away several years ago, the Wild Bird Center continues to help the native birds of the Florida Keys who find themselves injured and in need of a little human intervention to survive.

Florida Keys Wild Bird Rehabilitation Center Website:
www.keepthemflying.org

Travel Bit Number 29: Bridges Between the Keys

Perhaps the quintessential picture of the Overseas Highway is that of a bridge stretching across the water into the sunset, seemingly disappearing into the setting sun. Over its 113 miles (182 km), the Overseas Highway crosses 18.8 miles (30 km) of bridges. Put differently, you spend over 15 percent of the trip from Key Largo to Key West on bridges.

Today, there are 42 bridges on the Overseas Highway. The longest of these bridges is Seven Mile Bridge (Travel Bit Number 72), at just under seven miles (12 km) long. The shortest span, at 37 feet (11 m) long, is the Harris Gap Channel Bridge. Of the original railroad bridges built for the Overseas Railway, 23 remain. Most of these original bridges are now used or slated to be used as part of the Florida Keys Overseas Heritage Trail (Travel Bit Number 54), a multi-use trail for non-vehicular traffic and pedestrians. Three of these original railroad bridges have been named National Historic Sites: old Seven Mile Bridge, Bahia Honda Bridge, and Long Key Bridge.

When the Overseas Highway took over the Overseas Railway, many of the railroad bridges were converted to carry highway traffic. These converted bridges were extremely narrow and very dangerous. The best place to get an idea of how narrow the old road was is at old Seven Mile Bridge, where you can see the center line of the road and the complete lack of any shoulder or extra room for traffic on the bridge. Unfortunately, the bridge is under construction until 2021. In the meantime, a stop at any of the old bridges can provide some idea of the narrowness of the bridges—just imagine two lanes of traffic on them.

Perhaps the most dramatic of the old bridges is the Bahia Honda Bridge. While the railroad traversed the bridge at a low level and the bridge trusses rose high over the tracks, the highway could not fit between the railroad trusses. To solve this problem, the state constructed the Overseas Highway on top of the old Bahia Honda Bridge. This over-the-top construction created a vertigo-inducing drive above the ocean.

A project completed in 1982 replaced all of the original railroad bridges with those that currently house the Highway. The project required the construction or reconstruction of 37 bridges. Today, the bridges of the Overseas Highway remain a highlight of any trip down the road. For those who travel the highway from beginning to end without stopping, however, those bridges are the source of a moniker that is not a compliment: non-stop drivers are "Bridge Counters" and can make the trip through the Keys in approximately two hours. It should go without saying that this is not the recommended way to make the trip.

Travel Bit Number 30: Tavernier (Mile 91.9)

Tavernier is the southernmost of the Key Largo communities. Although most places in the Keys bear a name with English or Spanish origins, Tavernier has a distinctly French name. In French, "Tavernier" means "tavern keeper." This name is apt from a historical perspective. Even before modern-day tourism, famed naturalist and artist John James Audubon visited the Keys and found the area around Tavernier to be too noisy for his tastes, thanks to its bustling nightlife. (Travel Bit Number 45.)

Though the French name seems fitting based on the community's history, it could also be a mispronunciation of the Spanish "Cayo Tábano." The Spanish phrase translates to Horsefly Key, a name that is also very appropriate. The biting insects in the Keys can be large and found in unpleasant quantities.

Tavernier is one of the best places along the Overseas Highway to see homes and buildings from the era before the Labor Day Hurricane. (Travel Bit Number 41.) In the years since the hurricane, various residents of Tavernier have moved these pre-1935 buildings from their original locations throughout the Upper Keys to Tavernier, creating an unintentional collection of the early buildings of the Keys on Key Largo. The only better place to see these homes is Key West, which was not hit by the devastating Labor Day Hurricane.

Travel Bit Number 31: Pineapples in the Keys

During the 1800s, one of the biggest industries in the Keys was farming. With a tropical climate and easy ability to ship items up the eastern seaboard of the United States, the Keys grew not just tropical fruits, but staples like potatoes and tomatoes. By the late 1800s, though, the Keys were known for one crop in particular: the pineapple.

Many of the wreckers engaged in farming when there were no wrecks in the islands. The first pineapple plantation in the Keys was started on Key Largo by a wrecker looking for something to do in between wrecks. Within a few years, the Upper Keys produced 85 percent of the pineapples eaten in the United States. Plantation Key's name came from the pineapple plantations that once covered it. Planter, a town that once existed at the location of modern-day Tavernier, once shipped over a million crates of fruit each year. It was so important that it was the site of the only post office between Miami and Key West until the 20th Century. Plantations in the Keys grew using a slash and burn method, and new land had to be cleared every three to four years. In the Keys, where land is at a premium, this meant a pineapple plantation had a short lifespan.

When the Overseas Railway linked the Keys to the mainland, the pineapple business suffered; the railroad charged less to transport imported pineapples than those grown in the Keys. Thus, it became cheaper to ship Cuban pineapples to Key West and then on to the mainland via the railroad, thanks to the Railway's odd policy. Farmers in the Keys replaced the pineapples with key lime trees, but the introduction of the seedless Persian lime elsewhere wiped out the commercial key lime industry in the early 1900s. The Labor Day Hurricane destroyed nearly all of the remaining farming in the Keys. What farming was left after the hurricane was destroyed shortly thereafter by rising land values brought about by the completion of the Overseas Highway. Today, the only agriculture that exists in the Keys is of the sort practiced by gardeners in their backyards.

Travel Bit Number 32: Islamorada (91.0)

About 15 percent of the trip on the Overseas Highway is spent traversing Key Largo. After leaving Key Largo, the next island on the Overseas Highway heading south is Plantation Key, one of the four main islands that make up the community of Islamorada (pronounced "Is-La-Mo-Ra-Da"). The other three main islands that make up the community of Islamorada are Windley Key, Upper Matecumbe Key, and Lower Matecumbe Key. Three other smaller islands are also considered part of Islamorada: Indian Key (Travel Bit Number 44), Lignumvitae Key (Travel Bit Number 43) and Tea Table Key, a private island.

Islamorada, which means "Purple Islands" or "Island Home," depending on whom you ask, is known as the Sportfishing Capital of the World and boasts an impressive number of boats and marinas across its islands.

Islamorada was also the longtime home of the late Ted Williams, one of the greatest baseball players to ever play the game. Popular rumor has it that he only moved away because increasing traffic on the Overseas Highway was making it difficult for him to make left turns on the road. If you are trying to do the same on a busy day, you will quickly sympathize with this sentiment.

Islamorada was also the site of one of the more interesting incidents involving government employees in recent years. Several years ago, the wife of the islands' mayor suspected the mayor of cheating on her. After finding him with the suspected other woman, the wife hit her husband — with a golf cart.

Monroe County Tourist Development Council – Islamorada:
www.fla-keys.com/islamorada/

Travel Bit Number 33: Fishing in the Keys

Islamorada, as noted in Travel Bit Number 32, is referred to as the Sportfishing Capital of the World. The nickname supposedly arose because Islamorada is the site of more sportfishing records than any other single destination in the world. Its reputation as a stellar fishing locale is both well-known and well-established; one need only look at the many pictures of long-dead presidents that line the walls of local establishments to get a sense of its long-standing popularity.

Islamorada's popularity and productivity as a fishing spot owes much to its location. From Islamorada, one can quickly and easily fish both the deep waters of the Gulf Stream and Florida Strait, as well as the shallow, back-country waters of Florida Bay. Someone on a single day fishing trip out of Islamorada can easily hit both of these varied types of fishing, allowing him or her to catch anything from a sailfish or a marlin to bonefish and snapper in a matter of a few hours.

Travel Bit Number 34: Plantation Key Colony (Mile 90.1)

Plantation Key, the first island of Islamorada one reaches on the Overseas Highway heading south, is named after the pineapple plantations that used to provide the backbone of the island's economy. Plantation Key Colony, a subdivision on Plantation Key, looks like any other subdivision in the Florida Keys. However, in the middle of the subdivision, there is a small mound that appears out-of-place. This mound was built not by modern developers, but by the American Indians who originally populated the Keys.

Before Europeans arrived in the Florida Keys, two groups of American Indians periodically inhabited the islands: the Calusa and the Tequesta. The former are known to have lived in what we now know as the Everglades and the Keys. The latter made modern-day Miami and the Keys their home.

Not much is known of either group of American Indians. Neither group farmed, and both are known to have relied upon fishing as their primary form of sustenance. It appears that the two tribes traded off in their occupation of the Keys. While rich in fish, the lack of a significant water source anywhere in the Keys likely kept the islands from being permanently inhabited by either group. It is known that the Tequesta would come to the Keys during the height of the mosquito season. While the islands are home to many mosquitoes, the swampy lands of south Florida would have been far worse than the islands, where the ocean breezes would at least slightly decrease their numbers and annoyance.

Both the Calusa and the Tequesta died out within a few hundred years after the arrival of Europeans in the Caribbean. The Calusa were mostly killed off by disease and slavery raids by other American Indian tribes soon after the arrival of the Europeans. The Calusa who survived were re-settled in Cuba by the Spanish and died out or assimilated into the Cuban population. The Tequesta had disappeared by the time the Spanish traded Florida to the British in 1763. The more numerous Calusa had always dominated the Tequesta in what is today southern Florida, but both ended up meeting the same fate. Today, little evidence remains of either tribe, but the mound on Plantation Key is one of those reminders of who originally called the Florida Keys home — even if they were, like so many of its current residents, only there for part of the year.

Travel Bit Number 35: Key Limes

Although the Keys have great seafood and at one time provided nearly all the pineapples consumed on the East Coast of the United States (Travel Bit Number 31), today one food is more associated with the Keys than any other: the key lime, and more specifically, key lime pie.

The key lime is native to Southeast Asia, but the trees were naturalized in the Keys after the abandonment of the pineapple plantations. The ubiquitous green limes one sees in stores today are not key limes at all, but Persian limes. True key limes are about one to two inches around, with a peel that is closer to yellow than green. The fruit itself is bright green and quite seedy. Their taste is at once both sweeter and more bitter than Persian limes.

As for those small "Key Limes" one sees at the grocery store? Those are just small limes, typically from Mexico — unless you are visiting an unusually well-stocked grocery store, you are unlikely to find the real thing.

Today, there is very little commercial cultivation of true key limes. However, many are grown at homes throughout the Keys. The trees themselves are thorny, and they bear fruit year-round, though the primary season for key limes in the Keys is from May to September. During the season, you can sometimes purchase the fruits in the Keys.

As for Key Lime Pie, getting a slice of it while traveling through the islands is not just easy but almost required; the pie is sold throughout the Keys. Key lime pie has long been available in the Keys, as its history almost certainly dates back to the days of the wreckers. (Travel Bit Number 25). In those days, there would have been neither fresh milk nor refrigeration available to residents of the Keys. As the original recipes for key lime pie called for canned sweetened condensed milk and didn't require the pie to be refrigerated, it made a perfect dessert for the era. The tasty dessert remains incredibly popular despite the present day availability of both milk and refrigeration in the Keys. But it's not just a favorite dessert in the Keys. In 2006, the Florida Legislature made key lime pie the official pie of the state of Florida.

Travel Bit Number 36: Betsey the Lobster (Mile 86.7)

Islamorada is known for its sportfishing, but fishing is not just a recreational activity in the Keys. The spiny lobster — a species of lobster that is covered with spines to protect it from predators — is the largest commercial fishery in Florida. Dishes made from the spiny lobster can be found on menus throughout the islands.

The Spiny Lobster bears only a slight resemblance to its more well-known Maine cousins. Visitors to the Keys can see this difference for themselves thanks to Betsey, an anatomically correct, 30 foot (9 m) tall and 40 foot (12 m) long spiny lobster sculpture. Betsey inhabits a parking lot outside an outdoor market and artist community along the Overseas Highway. The ocean-dwelling version of the spiny lobster only grows to about two feet (.6 m) long and 15 pounds (6.8 kg). The most apparent anatomical difference between the spiny lobster and its northern cousin is the former's lack of large, front claws.

Betsey, who is about 30 years old, was created by Marathon artist Richard Blaze and is supposedly the second-most photographed site in the Florida Keys after the Southernmost Point buoy in Key West.

Depending on who you ask, Betsey may be the largest lobster in the world. Her competition for that title comes from Shediac, New Brunswick, a city known as "The Lobster Capital of the World." Their lobster statue — depicting the Maine version — is about 35 feet (11 m) long and 16 feet (5 m) tall. As one can see from a quick comparison, this is smaller than Betsey; however, the Shediac lobster weighs in at nearly 100 U.S. tons. Betsey weighs a mere fraction of that, and this weight discrepancy has caused Shediac to proclaim their lobster as the world's largest. The debate rages on, but either way, one will probably need a lot of butter to deal with either of them.

Travel Bit Number 37: Coral

Despite its appearance, coral is not a rock, but a living organism. In the same phylum as jellyfish and sea anemones, you can look closely at a coral and see that it has both tentacles and a mouth. A single living coral organism is quite small and called a "coral polyp." A single one of these polyps can range in size from the head of a pin to the size of a pencil eraser. Coral reefs are merely huge colonies of coral polyps, and while it may appear to be one large entity, a reef is actually made up of thousands of individual organisms.

The process of creating a coral reef is slow but simple. As a coral polyp grows, it secretes calcium carbonate. We like to think of this as coral polyp poop, even though this is not at all what it is. Calcium carbonate is not uncommon; limestone is also calcium carbonate.

After secreting it, the polyp sits upon this calcium carbonate, continuing to deposit more and more of it as it ages. The many thousands of polyps that can live in a colony grow and build the coral or coral reef up and outwards, with a foundation of calcium carbonate below. Different types of coral polyps make different types of what we think of as coral, from the long, cactus-like formations of a staghorn coral to the short, round formations of a brain coral.

On a piece of what is typically thought of as coral, only the outer 1/10 of an inch (2-3 mm) consists of living coral polyps. Hard corals in the Keys grow slowly—about ¼ to ½ an inch (1/2 to 1 cm) over the course of a year. Divers are discouraged from touching corals; this can sometimes kill either some or all of the entire colony of small coral polyps. With their slow growth rate, it can take decades to repair a coral formation that is even inadvertently disturbed or killed.

The Florida Reef exists at the absolute northern limit for a coral reef. Coral requires waters from 68-86 degrees

Fahrenheit (20-30° C); anything above or below that will starve and kill the coral reef in a process called coral bleaching. Coral reefs also require high water quality to survive, with a constant flow of nutrients and dissolved oxygen. The Florida Reef has both of these, but the temperature in winter is close to the lower limit of what a coral reef can withstand without being killed. Thanks to continuing conservation efforts, the Florida Reef is healthy today, but that health comes at the price of constant vigilance.

Stores throughout the Keys sell coral, but the coral they sell is not harvested in the Keys. All of the coral comes from reefs elsewhere in the world. Even though it comes from elsewhere, visitors to the Keys are discouraged from buying coral, as it increases pressure to destroy those coral reefs where harvesting occurs, even as the reef in the Keys continues to grow.

Travel Bit Number 38: Windley Key State Fossil Reef Geological Site (Mile 85.3)

Windley Key, part of Islamorada, used to be two islands — the Umbrella Keys. During construction of the Overseas Railway, the water between the two was filled, making the single island we know as Windley Key.

While the majority of state parks in the Keys are devoted to the preservation of nature, Windley Key is home to a natural preserve that only exists because of the intervention of man: the Windley Key State Fossil Reef Geological Site. Most of the islands in the Florida Keys are former coral reefs. During the construction of the Overseas Railway, Windley Key was the site of numerous quarries. The islands, being former coral reefs, consist of calcium carbonate — what most people know as limestone. Limestone was good fill for the approaches the railroad made to the islands of the Keys, as well as the bed of the railroad itself, and its quarrying was vital to the railroad's construction.

Once complete, the quarries might have shut down. However, the limestone from the quarries on Windley Key proved popular with builders on the mainland, who happily purchased this "Keystone" for buildings across the country. From homes in Miami and Key West to the St. Louis post office, the stone from Windley Key served to extend the life of the quarries long after the railroad had closed. The quarry that is now part of Windley Key State Fossil Reef Geological Site remained active until the 1960s.

After the closing of the quarries, the state gained control of the quarry that makes up the state park. Visitors to the Park can walk along the quarry walls to see a cross-section of rock and learn of the quarry's operation. As the name of the quarry implies, the limestone quarried here was home to many fossilized animals. Thanks to the quarry, you can now see the fossils in the layers of limestone exposed by the work of the quarry.

Florida State Parks – Windley Key Fossil Reef Geological State Park:
www.floridastateparks.org/park/Windley-Key

Travel Bit Number 39: Florida Keys National Marine Sanctuary

Designated on November 16, 1990 by President George H. W. Bush as a National Marine Sanctuary, the Florida Keys National Marine Sanctuary protects almost all of the waters around the Florida Keys. With a boundary designated as the high water mark, once you step foot in the waters around the Keys, you are likely in the National Marine Sanctuary. The main exception to this are the waters around the Dry Tortugas, which are protected as part of Dry Tortugas National Park, rather than the Marine Sanctuary.

Within the Marine Sanctuary, there are various levels of protection. These levels of protection are designed to both protect the waters of the Keys as well as allow for their recreational and commercial use. In places, the Marine Sanctuary has installed mooring buoys to prevent anchoring on the reefs; boats with divers can hook up with these buoys rather than anchoring in areas where their anchors could destroy fragile reefs. There are about five hundred of these buoys, saving coral from destruction on a daily basis.

For visitors to the Keys, the functions of the Marine Sanctuary likely happen in the background and are not noticed; however, the Sanctuary's efforts help provide the environment in which one enjoys the Keys, even if that effort goes entirely unnoticed.

National Oceanic and Atmospheric Administration – Florida Keys National Marine Sanctuary:
    floridakeys.noaa.gov

Travel Bit Number 40: Theater of the Sea (Mile 84.2)

You can find one of the more prominent tourist attractions in the Florida Keys on Windley Key: the Theater of the Sea. The second oldest marine mammal attraction in the world after Marineland of Florida near St. Augustine, Theater of the Sea is also one of the oldest tourist attractions in the Florida Keys. It opened in 1946 and would have opened earlier, but World War II halted plans to open it in the early 1940s.

As noted in Travel Bit Number 38, Windley Key was home to limestone quarries that provided stone to both the Overseas Railway and private individuals. When those quarries were abandoned one-by-one after the railroad's closing, they were not very valuable, as no one saw any purpose or use for the quarried land. Some did see value in the land or the land's potential, and those purchasers were able to obtain the property for almost nothing. For example, the land on which Theater of the Sea sits was purchased for $800. At the time, this was thought to be a bad deal—for the purchasers.

When it opened on the site of the former quarries, Theater of the Sea offered visitors a chance to see marine mammals up close and personal and proved very popular, particularly as there was almost nowhere else to do so. Several generations later, the park still allows visitors a chance to interact with sea animals up close.

Theater of the Sea Website:
    theaterofthesea.com

Travel Bit Number 41: The Labor Day Hurricane

In modern history, two events have shaped life in the Florida Keys more than any others: the construction of the Overseas Railway and the 1935 Labor Day Hurricane.

On September 2, 1935—Labor Day—the strongest, most intense hurricane to make landfall in the Atlantic Basin of the United States in recorded history hit the Florida Keys. Along with Hurricane Camille (1969) and Hurricane Andrew (1992), it is one of only three hurricanes to ever make landfall as a Category 5 storm in the United States. This hurricane is known as the Labor Day Hurricane or the 1935 Hurricane. Until the early-1950s, the naming of storms in the Atlantic Basin was an informal matter, if it occurred at all. This changed when, during the 1950 hurricane season, three large storms simultaneously appeared in the Atlantic Basin. Due to the confusion of differentiating these three potentially dangerous storms for residents, when the next storm arrived, it was given a name to ease its identification. The system of naming hurricanes in the Atlantic Basin was formally adopted before the 1951 hurricane season, long after the landfall of the 1935 Labor Day Hurricane.

The Labor Day Hurricane came onshore at modern-day Islamorada, hitting Upper Matecumbe Key, Lower Matecumbe Key, Long Key, and Craig Key hardest. With a storm surge of 17.5 feet (5 m) and winds gusting to 200 miles (320 km) per hour, the Labor Day Hurricane proved devastating, killing as many as 600 people. For perspective on the storm's surge, the highest natural point in the Florida Keys is 19 feet (6 m) above sea level.

On Upper Matecumbe Key, the hurricane proved particularly devastating. Once the storm passed, you could see from one end of the island to the other. Nothing on the island, from buildings to trees, remained standing. There was, however, one exception: an angel marking the grave of Etta Pinder. Etta had been the only child of one of the original families to settle the island. Etta passed away at a young age, and her family marked her gravesite with an angel. Etta's gravestone angel survived the storm, with only a broken wing to show for the devastation around it. Today, the angel is still standing on Upper Matecumbe Key in a pioneer cemetery and is known as "The Angel with the Broken Wing."

Most infamously, the Labor Day Hurricane killed over 200 veterans of WWI. When the hurricane hit, the veterans were working to build new bridges for the Overseas Highway as part of a Depression-era government work relief program. The work relief program housed the veterans in non-reinforced buildings, and most of those who died perished in or around their homes. At Mile 81.5, you can visit a large memorial to the veterans and others who died during the Labor Day Hurricane.

The most long-lasting effect of the Labor Day Hurricane was not the destruction it wrought, but the construction that grew out of it. When the hurricane hit, the Overseas Railway was in dire financial straits, having declared bankruptcy in the wake of the Great Depression. The Labor Day Hurricane destroyed or damaged major portions of the railroad. Unable to rebuild, the railroad sold its tracks and bridges to the state of Florida. Florida used the bridges of the old railroad to complete the Overseas Highway to Key West, finishing the road that, until then, had been reliant on ferries for much of its length.

Travel Bit Number 42: The Bonus Army

Many men who lost their jobs with the start of the Great Depression were veterans of World War I. These veterans had been awarded bonus certificates upon the completion of their service, but the certificates were not payable until 1945. Out of work and with families to feed and shelter, many of these veterans marched on Washington, D.C. during the spring and summer of 1932 to demand immediate payment of their bonuses.

Upon arriving in Washington, most of the men and their families camped in what is now Anacostia Park. A nearby dump provided the building materials/trash for this camp's construction. Ultimately, the protesters were forcibly driven out and removed from the property. Two of them were killed in an initial attempt to drive them from the park, and many were injured in a second, successful attempt to drive them off.

In 1932, President Roosevelt was elected and opposed paying the bonuses early. Instead, President Roosevelt issued an executive order that allowed 25,000 veterans to enter the newly-created Civilian Conservation Corps. These veterans could join the CCC without meeting the program's usual requirements to be single and under twenty-five.

A second, similar program allowed state emergency relief administrations to employ veterans identified by the Veterans Administration as needing work. The Federal Emergency Relief Administration offered grants to states for construction programs if they would hire these veteran laborers. This Federal Emergency Relief Administration program is how members of the Bonus Army ended up in the Florida Keys working on the construction of the Overseas Highway, where so many of them were killed in the Labor Day Hurricane. (Travel Bit Number 41.)

Travel Bit Number 43: Lignumvitae Key (Mile 78.5)

Lignumvitae Key is a small, uninhabited island which gets its name from the lignum vitae tree. First described in the 1400s, legend has it that the tree originally grew in the Garden of Eden. In the Bahamas and elsewhere in the Caribbean, the tree is often referred to as "Holywood," perhaps after the longstanding story that the Holy Grail was crafted from the wood of the tree.

Despite its considerable standing in legend, the lignum vitae tree itself is rather small, growing only to 30 feet (@ m) tall. It blooms in March or April, producing small, blue flowers; it later produces a small, orange-yellow fruit. While pretty, the lignum vitae's real value is found not in its attractive appearance. Instead, like the adage, it is what is inside the lignum vitae that counts; its wood is remarkable.

The wood of the lignum vitae is one of the densest — if not the densest — woods in the world. A piece of lignum vitae immediately sinks if dropped in the water. On this basis alone, the wood from the tree would be valued, but it has an additional feature that makes it valuable: it is also full of resin that keeps it from drying out once cut. Thus, lignum vitae has long been used in outfitting boats and bearings in submarines. The U.S.S. Nautilus, the world's first nuclear-powered submarine, had bearings constructed from lignum vitae wood; the resin in the bearings made them self-lubricating. Police batons were once made of lignum vitae wood thanks to its heavy weight, and its resin has been used as a remedy for syphilis and gout.

Today, like its neighbor Indian Key, Lignumvitae Key is part of the Florida State Park system. Lignumvitae State Botanical Park is home to the last untouched tropical hammock in Florida. Unlike most of the Keys, Lignumvitae Key never suffered fires or anything more than small-scale, personal farming. It hosts no invasive species of plants or animals, and the few that may have called the island home in the past have been eradicated. Although there have been human inhabitants on the island from time to time — including a Miami chemist who built the caretaker's home that serves as the visitor center for the State Park — the island is an oasis of the past in the modern Keys.

Lignumvitae Key is also home to a half-mile long, four foot (1.2 m) tall coral rock wall that is one of the most peculiar sites in the Keys. No one knows who built this wall or when they built it. As the island typically only had one resident family at a time, its large size is somewhat at odds with the known history of the island. How the wall got to Lignumvitae Key and who built the wall remains a mystery.

Florida State Parks - Lignumvitae Key Botanical State Park: www.floridastateparks.org/park/Lignumvitae-Key

Travel Bit Number 44: Indian Key (Mile 78.0)

One does not typically think of a ghost town in a tropical paradise. Indian Key, however, is home to just such a tropical ghost town. But it's not just any ghost town. This ghost of a town was once one of the largest cities in Florida and the seat of Dade County before Miami was anything more than a spit of land at the edge of a swamp.

In the 1830s, the wrecking industry (Travel Bit Number 25) was flourishing in the Florida Keys. One of the biggest wreckers — a man by the name of Jacob Housman — established himself on Indian Key. The decision to work from Indian Key was simple for Housman. By establishing himself at Indian Key, he could avoid the wrecking rules set and enforced by the government and court in Key West.

For a time, Housman and Indian Key flourished. As previously noted, Indian Key became the original county seat for Dade County, now the largest county, population-wise, in Florida. Indian Key boasted a hotel, a post office, wharves, warehouses, and even a bowling alley. John James Audubon visited Indian Key in 1832 — making him the first known tourist to visit the Florida Keys — and by all accounts thoroughly enjoyed himself on the island. His journals tell of a large party that took place during his visit, with music and copious drinking.

By 1840, Indian Key was home to dozens of people and was the second largest community in the Florida Keys after Key West. In an era where piracy still existed, and attacks by American Indians were still somewhat frequent, the only protection for the island came from the Navy's Florida Squadron. The Florida Squadron was also responsible for security elsewhere in the Keys. On August 7, 1840, the Florida Squadron was out of their home port at nearby Tea Table Key when a group of Seminoles invaded Indian Key, looking for the treasure they heard could be found on the island. The Seminoles burned nearly every house on the island to the ground and killed all of the island inhabitants they could find. The survivors hid in the island's cisterns and turtle kraals (corrals used to house turtles). The Seminoles slaughtered all those who didn't adequately hide. In the end, they killed sixteen people, and the survivors abandoned Indian Key.

Since the slaughter at Indian Key, there have been some small settlements on the island. During the 1870s, it was briefly used for boat building. During the 1930s and 1940s, treasure hunters dynamited much of the island in a search for the same hidden treasure sought by the Seminoles a century earlier. In the 1960s, marijuana smugglers found it to be a convenient hideaway. In 1971, the State of Florida purchased the island and turned it into Indian Key Archeological Site. Although part of Islamorada, today the island is inaccessible except by boat, and the state preserves it as a tropical island ghost town.

Indian Key Historic State Park:
        www.floridastateparks.org/park/Indian-Key

Travel Bit Number 45: John James Audubon

Born to a sea captain and his mistress in present-day Haiti, John James Audubon did not have an auspicious beginning to a life that would eventually result in *Birds of America*, a remarkable piece of ornithology and artistry that is still renowned today. His mother died shortly after his birth, and Audubon was raised in the islands by both his father's other mistress and in France by his father's wife. In both locations, Audubon developed an early love of birds. He arrived in the United States in 1803 on a false passport to escape the Napoleonic Wars. Moving to his father's landholding in Pennsylvania, Audubon found himself in a place he considered paradise, where he could observe and study the myriad birds of the new and mostly unexplored United States.

With a young family, Audubon continued moving west to newly opened lands. In 1826, Audubon took his drawings to England, where he published *Birds of America*, his crowning work. The work would be released over the years 1827-1838 and eventually featured 435 hand-colored prints of 497 species of birds. The work has become one of the most valuable collections ever printed. After adjusting for inflation, five of the ten highest prices ever paid at auction for books have been paid for *Birds of America*. Only 120 complete copies of *Birds of America* exist, and of those only 13 are privately-held.

As he completed *Birds of America*, Audubon made his way to the Keys. He is known as the first tourist ever to visit the islands. During his trip, Audubon collected and drew specimens for the book. In 1832, on his 47th birthday, Audubon landed on Indian Key (Travel Bit Number 44). He almost immediately saw his first flock of flamingos. During his week on Indian Key and the surrounding islands, Audubon would discover many birds he had never seen, including the roseate tern, the double-breasted cormorant, and the reddish egret. Audubon also traveled to Key West on his vacation to the Keys. The home where he stayed and worked is preserved as the Audubon House and Tropical Gardens, and it is open to visitors.

Travel Bit Number 46: Tarpon

Visitors to the Keys are treated to the sight of one type of fish more than any other: the tarpon (*Megalops atlanticus*). Measuring from four to eight feet (1.2 to 2.4 m) long and weighing 60-280 pounds (25-130 kg), tarpon are large fish. Visitors to the Keys who find themselves walking in the marinas can see their long, strong bodies slowly swimming beneath the docks. The fish are usually cruising the waters in search of handouts and the remnants of fish being cleaned. It is these handouts that make the tarpon a Keys tourist attraction in their own right. At various marinas throughout the islands, visitors can feed the tarpon or watch other braver (or foolhardier) souls feeding them. To see a fish weighing a quarter of a ton leaping out of the water to snatch a fish out of the hand of an unsuspecting tourist is unforgettable — particularly for the unsuspecting tourist.

Although tarpon feeding is the way most visitors to the Keys see tarpon, they are also a favorite fish for sportsmen. In addition to their size, tarpon are known to jump once they are hooked, providing a terrific fight for the man or woman on the other end of the line. While a great fighter, the tarpon is a bony fish and is rarely eaten. This means that sportsmen keep very few tarpon. Most people snap a picture with their catch and toss it back. The tarpon thus lives another day to fight another angler — or to surprise more unsuspecting tourists.

Florida Fish & Wildlife Conservation Commission – Tarpon Website:
myfwc.com/research/saltwater/tarpon/

Travel Bit Number 47: Snails

In the 1800s, the Florida Keys were home to an animal whose rare specimens were worth huge sums of money: the Florida Liguus Tree Snail (*Liguus fasciatus*).

At two inches long, these snails are a medium-sized snail that bear a beautiful shell. Their shells come in a variety of colors, from white to black, and nearly any color of the rainbow in between. The pattern on the shell varies from island to island throughout the Keys. On the larger islands, the shell pattern even varies from hammock to hammock. In other words, the shell of a snail from Upper Matecumbe Key will be of one pattern, while that of the snail from nearby Indian Key will be entirely different. There have been 58 color varieties described, though many are now extinct or very rare.

In the frenzy to collect these snail shells in the 1800s, collectors would go to any length to get a new and unusual pattern. One of the more common methods to keep a shell of a particular snail rare involved unscrupulous collectors procuring several examples of a snail from one island. The collectors would then burn the vegetation on the island to the ground. Tree snails spend their entire lives in trees except to lay eggs. Burning down an island would, therefore, result in the death of all the snails on that island. With all of the snails on an island thus killed — except, of course, the few specimens in the hands of the collector — the value of the remaining shells would be astronomical.

Despite the attempts (and sometimes successes) of the collectors to keep the snails rare, today tree snails live on many of the Florida Keys and throughout southern Florida. Like their predecessors that caused so much destruction during the snail collecting craze, these snails still retain considerable variations in color and pattern throughout the Keys. For example, the snails on No Name Key have a dark cream base, with brown and white banding. On Lignumvitae Key, the shells of the snails have a cream base as well, but the bands are red and green. Keep an eye out for these slow, curious residents of the Keys while on a hike. If you do, you are likely to be rewarded with the sight of one of the Keys' more colorful creatures—both physically and historically.

Travel Bit Number 48: The Boy Scouts' Florida Sea Base (Mile 73.8)

Today, just before the Channel Two Bridge, you catch a glimpse of the entrance of the Boy Scouts' Florida Sea Base. Here, Boy Scouts from across the United States come every year to learn to sail, snorkel, and enjoy the outdoor pursuits the Keys offer. The Florida Sea Base is one of four such locations owned and run by the Boy Scouts throughout the Caribbean.

The history of the site of the Boy Scouts' Sea Base is tied to the Labor Day Hurricane. Many World War I veterans who were working on the Overseas Highway when the storm struck were in a construction camp thought to have been located on or near the site of the present day Boy Scouts' Sea Base. This construction camp was known as Camp 3. Among the projects that these men were working on was a nearby bridge to be constructed for the Overseas Highway. When the hurricane hit, it killed many of these veterans and destroyed nearly everything they had constructed.

When crossing the Channel Two Bridge at Mile 73, just after the Sea Base, you can see eight concrete bridge pilings constructed by the vets on the Gulf side of the bridge. To the north-east of the pilings sits a small island, now known as Veterans Key. These pilings and Veterans Key — a manmade island — are all that remains of the work done by the World War I veterans on the Overseas Highway before the Hurricane. These works continue to be a poignant reminder of the destructive power of hurricanes and the lives of the veterans lost in the Labor Day Hurricane.

After the hurricane, the current location of Florida Sea Base became home to a fishing camp. The camp's location was dictated not so much by the excellent fishing in the area, but by the location of a toll at the Channel Two Bridge. Tourists and fishermen who didn't want to pay the toll could stop at the fishing camp. In the early 1950s, the fishing camp became the Tollgate Inn, which built a 300 foot (90 m) dock that could accommodate the largest fishing boats in the area. The toll booth and the Tollgate Inn are now gone, and the Boy Scouts purchased the latter in 1979.

Travel Bit Number 49: World War II in the Keys

During World War II, the Florida Keys became home to a significant military presence. With their beautiful weather, the Keys provided an excellent year-round base for training. Moreover, with the threat of German U-Boat attacks along the American coastline, the Keys' location proved crucial for preventing such attacks in the Gulf of Mexico.

While today the threat of U-Boats on the coast is nearly forgotten, at the beginning of World War II, these submarines regularly sank ships within sight of coastal residents. Twenty-four ships were sunk off the Florida coastline alone. Over the course of the summer of 1942, many of these ships were sunk in the Gulf of Mexico before the Navy could fully implement protection of the waters from Key West.

Although the last ship sunk by U-Boats in the Gulf of Mexico was in September 1942, attacks in the Atlantic continued, as did attempts to carry out attacks in the Gulf. On July 18, 1943, this resulted in a unique battle—the only recorded one of its type in history. On that summer day, about forty miles (65 km) southwest of Key West, a Navy blimp engaged a U-Boat in battle. The blimp delivered several depth charges on the sub, while the sub fired on the blimp. One of the shots from the U-Boat disabled the blimp's starboard engine, and it crashed into the waters of the Gulf Stream. One sailor on the blimp was killed, and the others spent twenty hours treading water and fending off attacks from sharks before their rescue.

Some numbers show the impact of the War on the Keys. The population of Key West increased from 13,000 to 45,000 over the course of the War. Additionally, the Navy's holdings on Key West and the neighboring islands jumped from 50 acres (20 ha) to 3,200 acres (1,295 ha). The increased military presence also led to improvements in infrastructure throughout the Keys. The Navy aided Florida in constructing the water pipeline that continues to provide water to residents of the Keys (Travel Bit Number 65) and built the 18 Mile Stretch of road to bypass the Card Sound Bridge and significantly cut the travel time needed to reach the Keys (Travel Bit Number 10).

Travel Bit Number 50: The Gulf Stream

The Gulf Stream is a powerful ocean current that begins off the tip of Florida and ends in the north Atlantic. The specific location of the Gulf Stream changes often, but it is usually about 60 miles (95 km) wide and 2,600-5,900 feet (790-1,800 m) deep, with a velocity of about 5.6 miles (9 km) per hour at its surface. Its deep blue water is easy to see from above when flying into the Keys, sitting offshore of the islands as it begins its long trek north.

Sailors have long known of the power of the Gulf Stream current and have taken advantage of it to speed their trips across the Atlantic. As early as 1513, Ponce de Léon noted the power of the Gulf Stream in his voyage's log. Early settlers in the Americas would go thousands of miles out of their way on Atlantic crossings to take advantage of the powerful current; the long detour was still faster than the trip with shorter mileage that did not take advantage of the Gulf Stream.

As for its name, that was partly due to Ben Franklin, who helped chart the current. His role in charting the current arose from his attempt to determine why mail traveling to the colonies from London took longer to arrive than it took for merchant ships to arrive traveling between the same two destinations. His investigation revealed that the government-run mail ship captains ran against the Gulf Stream current, while the merchant ship captains interested in speed and maximizing their profits crossed it, tracking the behavior of whales and their behavior in and around the current. The merchant ships could shave two weeks of travel time off of their trips, solely by taking advantage of the Gulf Stream.

Travel Bit Number 51: The Shipwreck Trail

Having been the site of over a thousand shipwrecks in the last 500 years and possessing a climate almost perfect for SCUBA diving, the Florida Keys National Marine Sanctuary has capitalized on that combination to create the Shipwreck Trail. The Shipwreck Trail is a series of nine ships whose wrecks span much of the last half millennium, and which are an excellent introduction to the types of wrecks found in the Keys.

The northernmost shipwreck on the Shipwreck Trail is the City of Washington. On July 10, 1917, east of Key Largo, she sank while being towed by a tugboat. Built in 1887, the City of Washington was in Havana Harbor on the night the U.S.S. Maine blew up, and she assisted in the rescue of survivors.

The Benwood is the next ship headed south; she sank on April 9, 1942, from a boat collision during World War II. On her last voyage, her lights were blacked out to avoid attack from the U-Boats that were patrolling the waters; this likely contributed to her sinking. (Travel Bit Number 49.)

The Duane is the next boat headed south; she is a purposely-sunk U.S. Coast Guard Cutter listed on the National Register of Historic Places. During World War II, the Duane sank the U-Boat U-77 and participated in four rescues at sea, ultimately saving 346 people.

The next boat, three miles northeast of the Alligator Reef Lighthouse, is the Eagle. The Eagle had been meant to be a purposely-sunk freighter, but she sank when she broke loose from her moorings before the scheduled sinking. The Eagle is now in two pieces, as Hurricane Georges split the ship in two in 1998.

Heading south is the oldest ship on the Shipwreck Trail, the San Pedro. The San Pedro, a member of the Spanish treasure fleet, sank in 1733 during a hurricane. Discovered in the 1960s, the San Pedro was found undersea with 16,000 silver pesos and Chinese porcelain that has since been recovered from the site. In only 18 feet (5.5 m) of water, snorkelers frequent the San Pedro.

The next sunken ship on the Shipwreck Trail is an unknown ship believed to be the Adelaide Baker, known locally as the Conrad. She wrecked four miles southeast of Duck Key as she headed for Savannah, Georgia with a load of timber. Wreckers rescued the captain and crew after the sinking of the ship.

Following the Adelaide Baker, headed south, is the Thunderbolt, another purposely-sunk ship. Built during World War II to plant and tend coastal minefields, the Thunderbolt—then called the Randolph—never saw action during the war. Florida Power and Light eventually acquired the Randolph and gave her the name she now bears. The name is a reference to her work on electrical energy research for Florida Power and Light.

The second to last ship on the Trail is believed to be the North America, a ship known to have sunk in the area in November 1842, while en route from Mobile to New York City.

The final ship along the Shipwreck Trail is the Amesbury. Located five miles west of Key West and locally known as Alexander's Wreck, the Amesbury sank after grounding while being towed to deep water for use as an artificial reef.

Florida Keys National Marine Sanctuary – Shipwreck Trail:
    floridakeys.noaa.gov/shipwrecktrail/welcome.html

Travel Bit Number 52: Upper, Middle, and Lower Keys

The Florida Keys are often divided into three distinct sets of islands: the Upper, Middle and Lower Keys. The Upper Keys stretch from the northern islands above Key Largo that don't have road access, through Islamorada and Lower Matecumbe Key. The Middle Keys run from Craig Key to Key Vaca. The Lower Keys are those from Little Duck Key past Key West and beyond the road to the Dry Tortugas.

Each of the sets of islands has its distinguishing features. The Upper Keys are known for their SCUBA and fishing. They are closer to the Gulf Stream and its warming waters than the rest of the Keys.

The Middle Keys are home to the three longest bridges in the Keys and are the parts of the Overseas Highway that one thinks of when imagining the road: the seemingly infinite vistas across the water from bridges high above the sea. The trip through the Middle Keys is what the author Juan Dos Passos called a "dreamlike journey," and thus it remains over a century after the Overseas Railway first crossed these Keys headed toward Key West.

The Lower Keys are home to the low, mangrove islands that the Overseas Highway quickly passes on the way to its end in Key West. (Travel Bit Number 101). They also include those islands beyond Key West, the Marquesas, and the Dry Tortugas. (Travel Bit Number 100.) Vacation homes and the military populate the Lower Keys. Throughout much of this portion of the Keys, there is a certain inevitability of the coming end of the road and an arrival in Key West, as if headed downhill.

Travel Bit Number 53: Fiesta Key (Mile 70.0)

With the arrival of the Overseas Highway, Fiesta Key — at the time called Jewfish Bush Key — became host to a resort with a motel, pool, store, restaurant and 300 campsites. In the era of the Overseas Railway, the as-yet-unwritten history of Fiesta Key looked much different; it owes its current fortune to the creation of the Overseas Highway after the Labor Day Hurricane.

Before the Labor Day Hurricane, what is now Fiesta Key had been bypassed by the Overseas Railway. This "bypass" was not extensive; the railroad passed only a few feet from Fiesta Key's shore but did not touch the island. This meant that there was no train station or ability to lure the tourist trade to Fiesta Key, despite the ability to practically touch a train while standing on the island.

When the original Overseas Highway was constructed before the Labor Day Hurricane, luck continued to pass by Fiesta Key. The ferries that connected much of the Highway did not stop at Fiesta Key. Instead, the ferries passed the small island at a distance. Fiesta Key looked like it would remain a small island with little future until the hurricane destroyed the railroad. The state constructed the new Overseas Highway across the island; the aforementioned resort quickly followed.

In 1947, the Greyhound Bus Company bought out the resort on Fiesta Key. Greyhound quickly changed the name of the Key from "Jewfish Bush Key" to "Tropical Key" and built a bus terminal and restaurant for passengers traveling between Miami and Key West. Almost as quickly as Greyhound had renamed the Key, locals gave it a new nickname: "Greyhound Key."

Two decades later, the island was sold again, this time to Kampgrounds of America, better known as KOA. They renamed it "Fiesta Key," a name that has stuck to this day. It is appropriate that Fiesta Key, with its history so tied to transportation across the Keys, should now be home to an RV resort.

Travel Bit Number 54: Florida Keys Overseas Heritage Trail

During the 1980s and 1990s, many of the original bridges that linked the Florida Keys were closed to both vehicular and pedestrian traffic. These bridges, constructed nearly a century earlier, were deemed unnecessary to the road or hazardous to those who would cross them and use them recreationally. Today, 23 of the original bridges constructed for the Overseas Railway remain, though many remain closed to all traffic, including pedestrians.

This state of affairs will soon come to an end, as the Florida Keys Overseas Heritage Trail is constructed to reconnect all the Keys via a multi-use trail from Mile 106 to the end of the Overseas Highway in Key West. Already underway, the Heritage Trail will ultimately provide a way for bicycles and pedestrians to travel the entire length of the Overseas Highway on dedicated trails separate from the Highway itself. Workers have already completed much of the trail; a significant amount of the work remaining involves re-linking the bridges of the Railway severed in previous decades. These reconstructed bridges will not only allow non-vehicular traffic to travel the length of the Keys but will allow for more fishing and sightseeing for those who want to get off of the road for a few hours or days.

Ultimately, the Heritage Trail will travel over 100 miles (160 km), through ten state parks. Even unfinished, and despite extensive damage to portions of the trail during Hurricane Irma, the Heritage Trail is already one of the busiest bicycle trails in Florida; its completion will likely make it the busiest. At the same time, the Heritage Trail will provide a welcome alternative for those who wish to see the Keys at a slower pace.

Florida State Parks – Florida Keys Overseas Heritage Trail:
www.floridastateparks.org/trail/Florida-Keys

Travel Bit Number 55: Long Key (Mile 67.5)

Long Key is an island with two distinct parts. The first part of the island that drivers headed south on the Overseas Highway encounter is well-populated and home to one of the few incorporated towns in the Keys: Layton. Layton is perhaps best known for its "speed trap." This speed trap is a police car permanently placed alongside the Highway, causing unsuspecting motorists to hit the brakes as they pass through town. This does not mean Layton has no working police cars. It is just that the one sitting conspicuously by the side of the road isn't one of them. Speeding is not advised in Layton or anywhere else in the Keys.

The second half of the island is almost entirely part of Long Key State Park. Long Key State Park has a very popular campground, known for its campsites overlooking the waters of the Gulf. Hurricane Irma struck Long Key State Park particularly hard, destroying its campground. As of early-2021, the state is still reconstructing the campground.

Spanish sailing charts called Long Key "Rattlesnake Key." Though there are rattlesnakes in the Keys (Travel Bit Number 85), they aren't common on Long Key. Instead, the name likely comes from the island's shape, which resembles a snake's head in the process of striking.

The first settlers on Long Key used it as a plantation for coconut palms. When the railroad arrived, the plantation became Long Key Fishing Camp (Travel Bit Number 56), a popular resort that played host to many a famous tourist before its destruction in the Labor Day Hurricane.

When leaving Long Key, the Overseas Highway travels the second largest water span in the Keys alongside the Long Key Viaduct. The viaduct was built for the Overseas Railway and consisted of 180 concrete arches across two and a half miles (4 km) of ocean. The Long Key Viaduct was Henry

Flagler's favorite bridge of all those along his railroad, and he featured it on many advertisements for the railroad. Today, the viaduct is part of the Overseas Heritage Trail. (Travel Bit Number 54).

Florida State Parks – Long Key State Park:
          www.floridastateparks.org/parks-and-trails/long-key-state-park

Travel Bit Number 56: Long Key Fishing Camp (Mile 65.8)

Before the Labor Day Hurricane, the Long Key Fishing Camp sat at the southwest end of Long Key. The Long Key Fishing Camp was a resort and center of recreation that served some of the most famous men of its day. Both Theodore and Franklin Roosevelt were known to have been guests, along with Herbert Hoover and William Hearst. With a 75 room hotel, cottages, a post office, and many boats and guides, the fishing camp was a luxurious way to enjoy the outdoor offerings of the Keys.

The Long Key Fishing Camp was also the winter home of Zane Grey, the famed author of novels on the American West. For 14 winters, Zane Grey fished and promoted the Florida Keys from the Long Key Fishing Camp, even serving as its president for three years. Grey was passionate about catch and release fishing, and the owners and promoters of the Long Key Fishing Camp shared that passion. The stated purpose of the Camp itself was: "To develop the best and finest hearts of sport, to restrict the killing of fish, to educate the inexperienced angler by helping them and to promote good fellowship."

The Long Key Fishing Camp thrived until the Labor Day Hurricane, which destroyed it. Briefly rebuilt in the 1960s, the location of the resort was later purchased by the state of Florida, which turned it into Long Key State Park. Very little of the original, pre-hurricane resort remains today. Near the ranger station for the park, however, is a unique remnant of the resort. A rusted section of a railroad passes near the ranger station, seeming to go nowhere. Surprisingly, it was not part of the Overseas Railway. Instead, it is a section of track that luggage trolleys once ran along, ferrying luggage from the actual railroad to the hotel and cottages of the resort's guests.

Travel Bit Number 57: Conchs – Part I

If key lime pie is the primary food associated with the Keys (Travel Bit Number 35), a close second would likely be the conch. "Conch" is a name applied to a number of large sea snails and their shells. Their meat is often used in foods in the Keys and the Caribbean, from salads and burgers to chowder and fritters. If you are eating conch in the Keys, it comes from one specific type of conch: the queen conch.

The queen conch lives in shallow, warm waters, either on a reef or in seagrass beds — both of which the Florida Keys have in abundance. Growing up to a foot (30 cm) long and living for up to 40 years, the Queen Conch has long been sought after in the waters of the Keys. The shells of the conchs were used by Native Americans for tools, jewelry, and cookware in and around the Keys long before the arrival of Europeans. And yes, conch shells were also used for blowing horns/trumpets. The first to use them in this way were likely Native Americans, but the wreckers famously used them as horns to signal a wreck ashore.

Unfortunately, the queen conch is vulnerable to overfishing. The juveniles have as much meat as the adults, and many juveniles are caught and eaten before they can reach reproductive age. In the waters of the Keys, it is illegal to catch a queen conch and has been for decades. Thus, all of the conch you eat in the Keys comes not from Florida, but from the Bahamas. Despite this ban, the United States continues to consume approximately 80 percent of the legal, internationally-traded conch.

Travel Bit Number 58: Conchs – Part II

A nickname often given to residents of the Keys—particularly the residents of Key West—is "Conch." People from Key West will tell you that the only people who should be considered true "Conchs" are those born in Key West. For much of the 1900s, though, this meant that nearly everyone born in the Keys was considered a Conch for one simple reason: there were no hospitals or midwives anywhere in the Keys except for Key West. If you were a baby born in a hospital or with the help of a midwife in the Keys, you were born in Key West, even if you lived elsewhere.

The "Conch" nickname extends to Key West High School, whose mascot is the Fighting Conch, and a local minor league baseball club also used the nickname.

During the 1700s and early-1800s, residents of the Bahamas regularly came to the Keys to fish, hunt turtles, and engage in wrecking. When the Key West federal court began to administer the wrecking industry, Bahamian residents who wished to continue wrecking in the Keys were forced to become American citizens, and many did so. These now former Bahamians settled in both Key West and the rest of the Keys. Throughout the islands, residents knew of the Bahamians' fondness for eating conch meat. (Travel Bit Number 91). The other residents of the Keys began referring to these former Bahamians as "Conchs," in what was likely a derogatory manner. Today, however, the term "Conch," as it refers to people, is used both endearingly and as a badge of honor for those who have always made the Keys their home.

Travel Bit Number 59: Duck Key (Mile 61.0)

Duck Key is an island on the ocean side of the Overseas Highway. The route of the Overseas Railway passed by the Key, as does the Overseas Highway. During the railroad era, Duck Key was a two-mile (3.2 km) long island and low lying, with a few small areas of mangroves and some other trees. Except for some salt manufacturing in the 1820s and 1830s, the island had been uninhabited throughout the written history of the Keys.

That changed in 1951 when a financier purchased the island. He had the idea of creating a grand resort and exclusive residential community. Before that could come to fruition though, a lot of work was necessary. To start, a bridge to the island from the Overseas Highway would be required. In 1952, the financier built a temporary wooden bridge; on the second day of 1953, a million dollar causeway to the island opened to traffic. Among the other projects undertaken in those early years of the island was the addition of 2.5 billion yards (2.3 billion m) of fill to the island, and the construction of four miles of canals through the island. Within the course of a few years, the island went from an isolated backwater to a major resort and residential community. All it took was a vision and a whole lot of money.

Travel Bit Number 60: Florida Bay

Between the Florida mainland and the Keys lies Florida Bay, a shallow patch of sea with an average depth of four to five feet (1.2 to 1.5 m). Scattered with small islands, Florida Bay is mostly part of the Everglades, though the portion closest to the Keys is part of the Florida Keys National Marine Sanctuary. Most of the Bay is shallow and is difficult to traverse by boat. Boat traffic in the area is thus regulated, and navigational channels have been dredged to allow boats to safely and responsibly cross the Bay.

Florida Bay is considered an estuary, which is a partially enclosed area where freshwater runoff meets the ocean. Here, that runoff is mostly from the Everglades. The estuary creates a gradual transition from freshwater to saltwater. In Florida Bay, that mix provides a home to a large variety of plants and animals, many of which are commercially or recreationally harvested.

Likely due to development around the Everglades, the amount of freshwater coming out of that swampland has been dramatically reduced over the years. The water of Florida Bay has become home to larger and more frequent algae blooms that kill marine species, as well as dead zones where nothing grows. Such changes are of little benefit to anyone, and researchers are working to determine what can be done to protect the valuable resource that is Florida Bay and its waters.

Travel Bit Number 61: Marathon (Mile 59.9)

Marathon, one of the three largest communities in the Florida Keys, began life as a base camp for railroad workers during the construction of the Overseas Railway. The name "Marathon" supposedly comes from the endurance of the workers who made Marathon their home.

Although many refer to the island on which Marathon sits as "Marathon," the island itself is named Key Vaca. The name "Key Vaca" likely has nothing to do with vacation, though its true origins remain unknown. One theory about its name is that it came from Alavar Nunez Cabeza de Vaca, a 16th Century explorer who was one of the earliest explorers of Florida. It is more likely that the name comes from the word "baca," which is Spanish for "cow." In this case, the term "cow" is not a reference to the farm animal, but to the "sea cow" or manatee. Manatees still ply the waters around the island. (Travel Bit Number 62.)

During World War II, the Army built an airstrip in Marathon as a training ground for the B-17 Flying Fortresses. The airstrip still runs alongside the Overseas Highway, though today it is mostly home to the private planes and jets of island residents and visitors.

Monroe County Tourist Development Council – Marathon:
www.fla-keys.com/marathon/

Travel Bit Number 62: Manatees

One of Florida's most famous animal residents makes its home in the Florida Keys: the manatee (*Trichechus manatus latirostris*). During the winter, manatees often head south looking for warmer waters than found in their northern summer homes. Manatees must have water temperatures above 60° Fahrenheit (15.5° C) to survive. The need for warm water is why those manatees which remain in northern parts of Florida gather near hot springs during the colder months. Winter is also the best time to see them in the Keys, as they slowly swim along the shore in the shallow waters, looking for food.

Manatees have long made the Keys home. A group of mangrove islands off of Plantation Key are called the Cowpens. The name comes from the manatee's "sea cow" nickname; they were once so numerous in this part of the Keys that they were herded into watery corrals in the Cowpens, where they could be easily killed and eaten. As noted in Travel Bit Number 61, the name of Key Vaca probably come out of their presence near the island.

Today, hunting of manatees in Florida is banned and has been since 1993. Still, nearly 40 percent of manatee deaths are caused by humans, whether due to manatees hit by boats or caught in fishing equipment. The curious creatures have little fear of humans and have difficulty hearing motors and avoiding boats as they near their feeding locations.

Florida Fish & Wildlife Conservation Commission – Florida Manatee:
    myfwc.com/wildlifehabitats/profiles/mammals/aquatic/
    florida-manatee/

Travel Bit Number 63: Mangroves

Across the world, there are 80 mangrove species. Mangroves are a recognizable tree thanks to their tangles of roots that often grow above ground. Mangroves are vital to many coastal areas, as they provide shelter to fish and wildlife while simultaneously stabilizing coastlines. In the Florida Keys, three species of mangroves line approximately 1,800 miles (2,900 km) of Florida Keys National Marine Sanctuary coastline.

The three types of mangroves found in the Keys are the red, black, and white mangrove. Often, all three are located close together. The red mangroves are the ones closest to the water, followed by the black mangroves and then the white mangroves as one moves onshore. In the Keys, the red mangroves are the ones that have the exposed root systems.

Freezing temperatures kill all three of the mangroves growing in the Keys. In theory, this means they should not be able to grow north of the Keys. However, thanks to the warm water of the Gulf Stream, mangroves stretch up both coasts of Florida and can survive temperatures which might otherwise kill them.

Florida Fish & Wildlife Conservation Commission – Mangrove Forests: myfwc.com/research/habitat/coastal-wetlands/ information/mangroves/

Travel Bit Number 64: Dolphin Research Center (Mile 59.0)

The waters around the Keys are home to many wild dolphins, but the most famous dolphin resident of the Keys spent most of her life at what today is known as the Dolphin Research Center. That dolphin was named Mitzi, but most people knew her as Flipper.

Today, the Dolphin Research Center is truly what its name states: a research center devoted to the study of dolphins. Open to the public, the center focuses its research on cognition, behavior, and husbandry of dolphins. However, this is not how it began life.

A local fisherman, Milton Santini, began what is now the Dolphin Research Center as a dolphin collection and training facility. Santini could get $100 per porpoise from aquariums and marine shows wanting to show off the animals to their paying crowds; he dynamited the Dolphin Research Center's lagoons out of the coral island and began a thriving business providing dolphins and porpoises to zoos and shows across the country.

Two years into Santini's operation, he caught a dolphin he named Mitzi. He had intended to sell her quickly, but while delivering six porpoises to Washington, Santini was in a car accident that killed several of the porpoises and broke his back. Laid up, Santini spent much of his time next to Mitzi's pool during his recuperation. While using a strength ball in his hand one day, he accidentally dropped the ball into the water. Mitzi immediately swam up and tossed it back to Santini. Intrigued, Santini threw the ball to Mitzi again, who once again quickly tossed it back to him with her snout, playing a dolphin version of fetch. In the days and weeks that followed, Santini realized how smart and easily trainable Mitzi was, and he started training dolphins. Santini quickly became one of the premier dolphin trainers in the country. As an example of the training he introduced, Santini was the first to train dolphins to do the backward tail walk that is now a ubiquitous feature of dolphin shows.

In 1963, Mitzi starred in the movie, "Flipper," the tale of a dolphin befriended by a fisherman's son. Although she didn't portray the dolphin in the television series that followed, she was, as they say, the originator of the role. In 1972, Mitzi passed away. She was buried at the Dolphin Research Center, and her grave is the first stop on tours of the Center, over 50 years after the movie that made her famous premiered.

Dolphin Research Center Official Website:
        www.dolphins.org

Travel Bit Number 65: The Water Pipe

The Florida Keys are almost entirely devoid of natural freshwater sources. There are no freshwater rivers or streams and save for a few small depressions that fill with rainwater, there are no freshwater ponds or lakes in the Keys, either. Over time, many of these few minor sources of rainwater dried up or were destroyed by development. With over 100,000 residents during the winter months, this lack of water poses a significant problem for anyone who makes the Keys home or just vacations there.

Until 1941, the primary way residents and visitors to the Keys obtained water was through the use of cisterns. The cistern collected the abundant rainfall of the islands and usually provided ample water for residents. During World War II, with more people in the islands for war training and defense of the Gulf of Mexico, the ability to ensure enough water for the residents of the Keys became a serious impediment to growth. To solve this burgeoning problem, the Navy and the state of Florida worked together to solve the problem of a lack of freshwater by constructing a pipeline from the mainland to Key West.

As originally constructed, the water pipeline to Key West held ten million gallons (38 million liters) of water. From its starting point on the mainland to Key West, it took six days for the water to travel the full length of the pipeline. Unfortunately for those at the end of the pipeline, water pressure after days of travel was less-than-ideal. Practically, this meant there was little to no water pressure on any second floor in Key West. Even after adding booster stations to the pipeline, which both increased water pressure and shortened the time it took to get water to Key West, second-floor water pressure was nearly non-existent for years.

Thankfully for today's residents and visitors to the

islands, the water pipeline now efficiently gets water to Key West, and even the tallest buildings can get water to their upper floors with plenty of pressure. There are storage facilities for freshwater along the way, should the pipeline ever be disrupted. There are also two desalination plants that can become an emergency source of three million gallons (11.3 million liters) of water per day for the Keys. You can sometimes see the pipeline along the side of the highway, such as when it crosses Grassy Key or along the underside of the bridges.

Travel Bit Number 66: Grassy Key Egg Farm (Mile 57.5)

Grassy Key used to be home to an egg farm with the not-so-creative name of Grassy Key Egg Farm. The farm provided the entirety of the Keys with eggs. However, it was probably more well-known as the place locals pointed to when attempting to give directions to the clothing optional beach.

The clothing optional beach that once existed near the Grassy Key Egg Farm is an example of why some consider the Keys — and in particular, Key West — as a location where anything goes. A few years ago, officers responded to an accident on Cudjoe Key. Upon asking the driver who caused the crash what had happened, she informed the officers that she had been shaving her bikini area while driving. While shaving, she had her passenger — who happened to be her ex-husband — take the wheel and steer. After further questioning, officers determined the driver was headed to Key West to meet her boyfriend and wanted to be ready for the visit. No word on how her ex-husband felt about the situation.

Travel Bit Number 67: Pirates in the Keys

The Florida Straits and the Gulf Stream were the primary shipping lanes of the Spanish Treasure Fleet. Better described as convoys, there were three of these fleets — called *"flotas"* in Spanish — that crossed the Atlantic Ocean between the Americas and Spain, and which regularly passed through the Florida Straits laden with treasure from the Americas for the Spanish crown. Less excitingly, the convoys also carried useful goods like food and lumber between the two continents.

The *flotas* mainly operated from the 1560s to the 1780s, and ultimately carried what would today be well over $500 billion in treasure. Because of the great wealth they carried, heavily armored companion ships protected the *flotas*. Despite the armored convoys, the *flotas* were often the target of pirates.

During the era of the *flotas*, the Keys provided an ideal place from which pirates could operate. The many shoals and islands of the Keys served as hiding spots, giving cover and protection from large ships seeking to follow or destroy the pirate operations. Only a few miles from the primary shipping lane of the *flotas*, the Keys were also conveniently located. For 200 years, the Spanish sought out pirates in the Florida Keys, hoping to protect the vast wealth flowing from the Americas back to Spain.

The pirates operated in search of treasure, but they also took prisoners from the ships they plundered. These prisoners were sometimes ransomed, but they were just as likely to be sold into slavery. The first wreckers (Travel Bit Number 25) in the Keys were likely pirates. They could comb the beaches and shallow waters for treasures and loot from wrecked ships and keep that plunder for themselves. Even a former slave, Black Caesar, made the Keys his home base for piracy. (Travel Bit

Number 16.)

   After the *flotas* ceased their treasure runs, pirates still roamed the Keys. In the 1820s, Commodore David Porter arrived in the Keys to deal with the continuing problem of piracy. Commodore Porter was a captain in the U.S. Navy who gained the honorary title of Commodore through his service to the United States during several wars and smaller military engagements. With a more significant military presence in the Keys, piracy eventually died out.

Travel Bit Number 68: Curry Hammock State Park and the Florida Circumnavigational Saltwater Paddling Trail (Mile 56.0)

Curry Hammock State Park, a park that features mangrove swamps, rockland hammocks, and seagrass beds stretching across several islands, is the largest uninhabited piece of land between Key Largo and Big Pine Key. The park is named for a Miami teacher whose father owned the land before its use as a park.

For those looking for an adventure, the Florida Circumnavigational Saltwater Paddling Trail passes through the waters of Curry Hammock State Park. As implied by its name, this 1,515 mile (2,440 km) sea kayaking route circumnavigates the state of Florida, traveling from Big Lagoon State Park near Pensacola on the Florida Panhandle to Fort Clinch State Park, on the Florida-Georgia border. If one were to drive between the start and end point of the trail, it would only be a 400 mile (640 km) journey, over 1,100 miles (1,800 km) shorter than the sea route.

Over its many miles, the trail traverses twenty national parks, seashores, wildlife refuges and marine sanctuaries, crosses 37 Florida aquatic preserves, and passes through 47 state parks, including Curry Hammock. Traveling the entire length of the trail typically takes three to six months, and only a few individuals have completed it.

Florida State Parks – Curry Hammock State Park:
www.floridastateparks.org/park/Curry-Hammock

Florida Office of Greenway & Trails – Florida Circumnavigational Saltwater Paddling Trail:
www.floridadep.gov/parks/ogt/content/
florida-circumnavigational-saltwater-paddling-trail

Travel Bit Number 69: The Reef Lighthouses

In the mid-1800s, with wrecks on the reefs around the Keys becoming a weekly occurrence, it became imperative to construct lighthouses to decrease the difficulties encountered by ships passing near the Florida Reef. Between 1852 and 1880, six lighthouses were erected to mark the reef off the Keys.

Construction of the lighthouses was challenging, to say the least. Early efforts to use lightships to mark the reefs often ended badly, with the lightships themselves wrecking on the very reefs and shoals about which they had been launched to warn. Eventually, an open skeleton design for the base of the lighthouses was determined to be an effective design. This design allowed the free flow of water beneath the lighthouse and offered less resistance during hurricanes to both wind and water.

Fowey Rocks Lighthouse — the "Eye of Miami" — is the northernmost lighthouse on the Florida Reef and was originally constructed in 1878. During the construction of Fowey Rocks Lighthouse, ships would regularly wreck on the reefs only a few feet from the lighthouse; construction workers often had to scramble to avoid the ships as they wrecked.

Carysfort Reef and Alligator Reef are the next two lighthouses headed south. The former was built in 1852, and the latter in 1873. Alligator Reef Lighthouse survived a direct hit from the Labor Day Hurricane and was undamaged by the twenty foot (6 m) wave that washed over it and destroyed the islands behind it.

Sombrero Lighthouse guards the shores off of Marathon and is the tallest of the six lighthouses at 140 feet (42 m). George Gordon Meade — later Major General Meade, who defeated General Robert E. Lee at the Battle of Gettysburg during the Civil War — oversaw the construction of Sombrero

Lighthouse in 1858 as part of his pre-war duties.

The final two lighthouses on the Florida Reef are American Shoal and Sand Key. The latter is about eight miles (13 km) southwest of Key West. With a light that projects up to 19 miles (30 km), you can sometimes see Sand Key Lighthouse from the city. American Shoal Lighthouse sits off of Cudjoe Key and in 1880, it was the last of the Reef lighthouses to be completed. The completion of American Shoal Lighthouse marked the end of the era of the wreckers, as its light warned ships off of the last portion of the Keys where wrecks regularly occurred.

Travel Bit Number 70: Crane Point Hammock Museum & Nature Trail (Mile 50.5)

Marathon is home to the Crane Point Hammock Museum & Nature Trail, a 63 acre (25 ha) preserve run by a non-profit foundation. Like so many of the preserves and parks in the Florida Keys, Crane Point was slated for development as private homes and a shopping center when the foundation stepped in to purchase the acreage in 1989.

Today, Crane Point is home to numerous features making it worth a visit. The property is home to the Adderley House, the oldest home in the Keys outside of Key West. A children's museum provides information for kids on the Keys, while adults can learn more about the history of Keys at the Museum of Natural History on the property. You can also visit the Marathon Wild Bird Center at Crane Point. They have rehabilitated and released over 16,000 wild birds since 1995.

Perhaps the best reason to visit Crane Point, though, is for its natural features. Crane Point has 2.5 miles (4 km) of trails and walkways. These take visitors through hammocks, a mangrove forest, tidal lagoons, a butterfly meadow and wetland ponds. Those who want to spend some time on the water can also take kayak tours of the property.

Crane Point Hammock Museum & Nature Trail Website:
www.cranepoint.net

Travel Bit Number 71: The Turtle Hospital (Mile 48.5)

The waters around the Florida Keys are home to five of the seven species of sea turtle: Green, Loggerhead, Kemp's Ridley, Hawksbill, and Leatherback. Turtles are opportunistic feeders and will eat almost anything. Their predilection for eating anything and everything has given sea turtles the nickname of "the goat of the sea." Unfortunately, these eating habits mean that sea turtles often find themselves with intestinal blockages or entangled in fishing and buoy lines. Although much has been done to help turtles — such as adding fishing line recycling bins at every single fishing bridge, beach, and marina in the Florida Keys — turtles still regularly find themselves victims of injuries indirectly caused by humans.

In the Florida Keys, this is when the Turtle Hospital steps in. Opened in 1986, the Turtle Hospital has four goals: (1) rehabilitate injured sea turtles and release them back into the wild; (2) educate the public; (3) conduct and assist in sea turtle research; and (4) work toward legislation to make beaches and water safe and clean for sea turtles. Since opening, the Turtle Hospital has released over 1,500 turtles back into the wild. The Turtle Hospital is open daily for people who want to learn more about sea turtles and the work being done in the Florida Keys to help these threatened and endangered species survive and, hopefully, thrive for many years to come.

The Turtle Hospital Website:
www.turtlehospital.org

Travel Bit Number 72: Seven Mile Bridge (Mile 47.0)

Of all the stretches of the Overseas Highway, perhaps none is more famous than the Seven Mile Bridge. Seven Mile Bridge is the longest bridge on the Highway and connects Knight's Key with Little Duck Key. Today, there are two Seven Mile Bridges. The first is New Seven Mile Bridge, the bridge that cars traveling the Overseas Highway use. It was completed in 1982 and is a wide, modern expanse of highway that is just under seven miles long.

The second bridge is Old Seven Mile Bridge, which was completed in 1912 as the longest bridge on the Overseas Railway. This part of the trip down the Overseas Highway was one of the stretches of road that the highway bypassed by ferries before the Labor Day Hurricane. (Travel Bit Number 41.) After the hurricane and the purchase of the Overseas Railway by the state of Florida, Old Seven Mile Bridge — which remained intact — would be converted to a highway bridge. The completion of Seven Mile Bridge would finally allow the highway to stretch from the mainland to Key West without the need for a ferry. Before vehicles could use the bridge, however, it needed to be widened. Eventually, the road was widened from 14 feet to 22 feet (4 to 6.7 m). Some of the railroad track pulled up from the bridge was used for much-needed guardrails on the repurposed bridge; the guardrails had been unnecessary when the bridge was limited to railroad traffic.

Normally, visitors can walk about two and a half miles (4 km) of Old Seven Mile Bridge and see the guardrails made of the old railroad tracks. While this is a fascinating bit of history, perhaps more fascinating is how narrow the road across Old Seven Mile Bridge was, even after its widening. The road markings — still visible on the bridge — show the narrowness of the road. It was not a road for the faint of heart. This portion of Old Seven Mile Bridge is currently undergoing repairs, and it is not open to foot traffic. Its reopening is planned for 2021.

After the opening of the New Seven Mile Bridge, many spans of Old Seven Mile Bridge were destroyed to allow boat traffic to pass through unimpeded. Today, one cannot walk across the entirety of Old Seven Mile Bridge because of these large gaps between spans. However, in 2014, the Florida Department of Transportation approved a plan to restore Old Seven Mile Bridge for bicycle and foot traffic. Once completed, Old Seven Mile Bridge will become part of the Florida Keys Overseas Heritage Trail. (Travel Bit Number 54.)

Travel Bit Number 73: Pelicans

Perhaps the most ubiquitous bird along the Overseas Highway is the pelican. These tanks of the sky float alongside the Highway's bridges and keep watch over its asphalt from perches above the water. Pelicans are the second longest birds in North America, after the trumpeter swan. They also have the second largest wingspan of North America's birds, after the California condor. Thanks to their large size, pelicans are a hard bird to miss along the road.

Two types of pelicans inhabit the Keys: brown pelicans (*Pelecanus occidentalis*) and white pelicans (*Pelecanus erythrorhynchos*). The white pelicans are, like many of their retired human counterparts, only seasonal visitors to the Keys. White pelicans spend their summers in the northern United States and southern Canada. They return each winter to enjoy the weather and abundant fish. The brown pelicans are year-round residents, as their tans can attest. Just kidding. Those are not tans. Pelicans know better than to sunbathe. They do not want to get skin cancer.

If you are interested in seeing pelicans up close, you can almost always find them where fish are being cleaned, attempting to grab any bones and portions of the fish that are not being sent home as food for humans. Up close, you can see the throat pouches in which they hold food being used for just that purpose, as well as get an idea of their large size.

Florida Fish & Wildlife Conservation Commission – American White Pelican:
> myfwc.com/wildlifehabitats/profiles/birds/shorebirdsseabirds/american-white-pelican

Florida Fish & Wildlife Conservation Commission – Brown Pelican:
> myfwc.com/wildlifehabitats/profiles/birds/shorebirdsseabirds/brown-pelican

Travel Bit Number 74: Pigeon Key (Mile 44.8)

In between the spans of the New and Old Seven Mile Bridges, approximately two miles (3.2 km) from the start of the bridges on Knights Key, lies a four-acre (1.6 ha) island called Pigeon Key. Passing it on the road, you can see a small group of buildings on the island, as well as numerous palm trees swaying in the ocean breezes. Many people have no idea who lives on the island or the island's purpose.

During the construction of Old Seven Mile Bridge for the Overseas Railway, Pigeon Key was home to hundreds of workers who were constructing the long bridge. These workers lived in pre-fabricated houses which were disassembled after the construction of the bridge was completed. The buildings that remain on Pigeon Key today were constructed from 1912-1920. These were built as homes for workers on the completed Overseas Railway, such as maintenance men and painters, who could live on the island with their families. These workers called Pigeon Key home until the destruction of the Overseas Railway in the Labor Day Hurricane.

During World War II, the island again proved useful when it became a training center for the armed forces. After the war, scientists from the University of Miami used the island as a home for experiments on raising sewage-eating fish, such as the tilapia. The tilapia is not native to the Keys, but it has displaced many other fish in the Everglades. Sea World eventually took over the island and used it as a staging area for collecting tropical fish from the waters around the Keys. Today, the Pigeon Key Foundation, a private non-profit, runs the island and provides camps and educational programs for students, as well as historical tours of the island.

Travel Bit Number 75: Cuba

Once you reach the Lower Keys, you are a mere ninety miles (145 km) from Cuba, which makes locations such as Key West closer to Cuba than they are to Miami or the mainland. Thanks to this proximity, the relationship between the Florida Keys and Cuba has a long history. From the earliest European exploration of the Caribbean, the proximity of the Florida Keys to Cuba has been highlighted in the shipwrecks that pepper the waters of the islands. Most of the wrecks in the Keys befell Spanish ships as they traveled from Havana to Spain.

In 1762, the Spanish traded Florida to Great Britain. However, the parties could not agree whether the Keys were part of Florida, and they made no provision for their trade in the agreement. For years, the question of who owned the Keys remained open. The Spanish did not concede that the islands were included in the trade, as many of the Keys were closer to Spain's Cuban lands than they were to the rest of Florida. The British and Spanish never officially settled the issue of the ownership of the Keys. However, when the United States took possession of Cuba as a protectorate after the Spanish-American War, it became a moot point. Long before that War, most of the Spaniards who made the Keys home had moved to Cuba, and Americans and transplanted Bahamians populated the Keys.

In more recent times, Cubans fleeing their island have frequently washed ashore in the Keys, risking their lives to escape to the United States. Some Cubans have made more dramatic entrances into the United States, going so far as to fly jets to the Naval Air Station in Key West. (Travel Bit Number 94.) A story—perhaps apocryphal—tells of Cuban soldiers who washed ashore in Key West, and strolled down Duval Street, attempting to seek asylum. No one in Key West seemed to see anything out-of-the-ordinary in the soldiers walking down the street in full combat gear, carrying automatic weapons. It took the soldiers hours to find help, either because everyone in Key West assumed the soldiers were wearing costumes, or because they did not even notice the soldiers among the not quite normal residents and visitors to the island.

Travel Bit Number 76: Iguanas

Sometime in the 1960s, the first green iguana showed up in the Florida Keys. The green iguana (*Iguana iguana*), a native of Central America, South America, and some parts of the Caribbean, is not native to the Florida Keys, but it has thrived since its introduction. No one knows how many there are in the Keys, but estimates range from tens of thousands to hundreds of thousands. They are often known as the rat of the reptile kingdom, in part because of their ability to populate an area quickly and easily.

The green iguana is the largest species of lizard, with males growing to be up to six feet (1.8 m) long, with a weight of over 20 pounds (9 kg). The green iguana is entirely a herbivore and can live to be well over 20 years old. Although many think of iguanas as pets, they are not necessarily good ones. Being so large, they require a large space to live. Despite a calm demeanor, they can take months or even years to tame. Moreover, they are poop machines. The average iguana poops up to a pound (450 g) a day, which is the same as generated by a medium- to large-sized dog.

Though the iguanas are shy, they are relatively easy to find if you are calm and quiet. They can be seen sunning themselves or just strolling among the quiet streets and trails of the islands. As an invasive species, the green iguana has caused problems in the Keys. It eats the gardens, flowers, and fruit trees of residents and may well have helped lead to the near extinction of the Miami Blue Butterfly. (Travel Bit Number 78.) Residents of the Keys have been known to shoot at the troublesome creatures, though this is not the recommended removal method.

Florida Fish & Wildlife Conservation Commission – Green Iguana:
myfwc.com/wildlifehabitats/profiles/reptiles/green-iguana/

Travel Bit Number 77: Bahia Honda State Park (Mile 36.8)

Bahia Honda Key is almost entirely part of Bahia Honda State Park, home to what is often considered the best beach in the Florida Keys. The island's name is Spanish for "Deep Bay," and the deep waters from which it gets its name allow more pounding of the island by waves, creating the natural beach that draws many tourists to Bahia Honda throughout the year. Hurricane Irma significantly altered the beach. As of the 2019 update to this edition of the book, most of the beach remains closed as do some of the park services, though the park is working to restore everything to its pre-hurricane beauty.

When leaving Bahia Honda Key headed toward Key West, it is impossible to miss the old railroad bridge that rises to the south of the current path of the Overseas Highway. Rising out of the ocean, you can walk out onto the old bridge from Bahia Honda State Park and get a beautiful view of the islands and ocean beyond. This steel bridge was the most difficult bridge to construct on the Overseas Railway. Not only is the current through the channel the fastest in the Keys, but the tidal surges during storms are also higher through the channel than elsewhere. As a result, the bridge had to be taller than any other in the Keys.

Before the construction of the current highway bridge in 1972, the Overseas Highway traversed the channel by the old railroad bridge. As a truss bridge, the railroad passed through the bridge at its lowest level; the support beams traveled above the railroad cars, providing support for the bridge itself. However, this presented a problem during the conversion of the bridge to use as a highway. The narrow path of the railroad bed was not wide enough for two lanes of cars, and the steel structure of the bridge couldn't be altered, or it would destroy the bridge's integrity. Rather than construct a new bridge between Bahia Honda Key and Spanish Harbor Key during the conversion of the bridges from the railroad to vehicular traffic, the decision was made to run the new Highway over the top of the old Bahia Honda Bridge. This decision created the most terrifying bridge crossing of all those along the Overseas Highway. The vehicle bridge crossed the deep channel from hundreds of feet above the water. Unsurprisingly, when the modernization of the bridges on the Overseas Highway began, the Bahia Honda Bridge was one of the first bridges to be replaced.

Florida State Parks – Bahia Honda State Park:
> www.floridastateparks.org/park/Bahia-Honda

Travel Bit Number 78: The Miami Blue Butterfly

Hurricane Andrew, one of the largest hurricanes to ever hit the United States, struck southern Florida in 1992. Among the assumed casualties of the storm was the Miami Blue Butterfly, a small blue butterfly that was once common from northeastern Florida to the Keys. Already nearly extinct in 1992 thanks to depletion of its natural habitat, when Hurricane Andrew made landfall, the hurricane was thought to have destroyed what little population of the Miami Blue that remained.

Then, in 1999, a population of about fifty Miami Blues was found in Bahia Honda State Park—the presumed extinction of the butterfly had not happened. The butterflies received protection, and their number swelled to 1,000. The University of Florida began a captive breeding program and has started a reintroduction program that, unfortunately, has yet to prove successful. In 2006, several other small colonies of the Miami Blue were found scattered throughout the Keys, indicating that the Bahia Honda colony was not the only one to have survived Hurricane Andrew.

The finding of this colony of Miami Blues and the establishment of the captive breeding program ultimately saved the Miami Blue population a second time. In 2010, all of the Miami Blues on Bahia Honda inexplicably disappeared. The reason is not known, but the suspected culprit is the iguana. (Travel Bit Number 76.) While not proved, scientists believe that the iguanas eat the leaves where the butterflies lay their eggs.

Today, the Miami Blue remains on the brink of extinction, though it is hoped that the reintroduction program will one day re-establish the Miami Blue throughout its former range. Those who see a Miami Blue should consider themselves lucky; it is likely the most endangered insect species in the United States.

Travel Bit Number 79: National Key Deer Wildlife Refuge (Mile 33.7)

At eight miles (13 km) long and two miles (3 km) wide, Big Pine Key is the second largest of the Keys after Key Largo. Big Pine Key is also the headquarters of the National Key Deer Wildlife Refuge, a refuge established in 1957 to protect the key deer.

Depending on whom you ask, the key deer is either a subspecies of the white-tailed deer or its own species. Unlike the white-tailed deer seen elsewhere in the United States, the key deer has one very noticeable difference: it is a deer in miniature form. At only two and a half feet (.7 m) tall and less than 75 pounds (34 kg), the key deer is less than half the size of a typical white-tailed deer. The fawns are only two to four pounds (.9 to 1.8 kg) at birth, and their hooves leave fingerprint-sized prints in the ground.

When first discovered by the Spanish in 1575, the Spanish found key deer on most of the Middle Keys and even on Key West. The Spanish used the small deer as a food source, and their population decreased as they and subsequent visitors and residents on the islands did the same. The deer's wide range in an era before the bridges was a result of their ability to swim. Although most deer and their relatives can swim, key deer seem to be the best swimmers in the deer family. Despite their initial range throughout much of the Keys, by the 1940s, fewer than 50 Key Deer remained.

Today, the population of key deer hovers around 1,000 animals. About 75 percent of the key deer are on Big Pine Key and its nearby neighbor, No Name Key. Both of these Keys are well-populated by humans, who are usually happy to put up with the deer in their yards. During Hurricane Irma, Big Pine Key suffered significant damage. However, the key deer made it through with little trouble.

If you are traveling down the Overseas Highway, you cannot fail to miss the signs warning travelers to slow down as they arrive on Big Pine Key. To keep the key deer from being killed on the Highway — their primary cause of death — the road is elevated across much of Big Pine Key. Unfortunately, 30 to 40 key deer still die on the road each year.

Thanks to the efforts of many to preserve the key deer, it is likely at its highest sustainable population on Big Pine Key and No Name Key. Efforts to reintroduce the animal on other Keys have begun. One day, the key deer may roam throughout the Middle and Upper Keys. For now, if you want to see this unique mammal, the best place to do so is on Big Pine Key and No Name Key.

U.S. Fish & Wildlife Service – National Key Deer Refuge: www.fws.gov/refuge/National_Key_Deer_Refuge

Travel Bit Number 80: The Southern Cross

The Southern Cross is a constellation that is ubiquitous in the southern hemisphere; it even appears on the flags of five nations in the southern hemisphere (Australia, Brazil, New Zealand, Papua New Guinea, and Samoa). Though known to be a southern hemisphere constellation, it is actually visible as far as 26 degrees latitude north. This means that along with South Texas and Hawaii, one of the three places in the United States where the Southern Cross is visible is the Florida Keys.

Although the Southern Cross never gets much above the horizon in the Keys, during the winter and spring months, it briefly rises above the horizon for part of the evening or morning. The Keys have proved themselves an excellent place to view the Southern Cross. On Big Pine Key, one example of a great place to stargaze, artificial light in the evenings is restricted because of the turtle nesting sites on the island. This lighting restriction, coupled with a lack of pollution in the Keys, makes for better stargazing than many other populated places.

Travel Bit Number 81: The Blue Hole (Mile 30.5)

In addition to being home to the key deer, Big Pine Key is also home to a rare sight in the Florida Keys: the alligator. These common Florida residents—and uncommon Keys inhabitants—make their home at an old quarry known as the Blue Hole.

As a manmade creation, the Blue Hole has no outlet. The water in the Blue Hole is rainwater. The Blue Hole is thus a rarity: it is a freshwater body of water in the Keys. As such, the Blue Hole attracts a variety of wildlife from key deer to iguanas, snakes, and birds. Here, they can almost always count on its waters for freshwater.

The only time the Blue Hole is not a source of freshwater is during or after a large storm or hurricane when storm surges of saltwater wash over the island. In 2005, the storm surge from Hurricane Wilma washed over Big Pine Key and deposited not just a significant amount of saltwater in the Blue Hole, but a number of saltwater fish as well. This saltwater would not harm alligators. While they are reptiles typically found in freshwater, they can survive in saltwater. The fish were a different story, as most suspected the fresh water that would eventually replace the saltwater would kill them. However, these saltwater fish, like the alligators, survived. Today, the Blue Hole is home to not just freshwater alligators, but saltwater tarpon and barracuda.

Those wishing to see the residents of the Blue Hole—particularly the alligators—are encouraged to bring binoculars, and use caution when near the water, lest one of the gators decide it would like a human snack.

Travel Bit Number 82: Mosquitos

Southern Florida — much of it a natural swamp — is known for its many mosquitos. The Florida Keys, while not a swamp, are also besieged by these insects. Among the many difficulties faced by people living in the Keys throughout the years has been the presence of the mosquitos that carry tropical diseases. These diseases are rare or otherwise not found in the rest of the United States.

Before the arrival of the water pipe (Travel Bit Number 65), most people in the Keys obtained their water by collecting it in cisterns. This standing water in the cisterns was a prime mosquito breeding ground. To counter the mosquito threat, officials dumped gambusia — a small fish known to feed on mosquito eggs — into the cisterns. On Big Pine Key, officials built mosquito ditches, into which they placed gambusia who could eat mosquitos all day and night.

Even with modern technology, medicines, and the pipeline, efforts to keep the mosquitos at bay remain constant in the Keys. There is an official Florida Keys Mosquito Control District that employs 71 full-time employees and 29 part-time employees; it exists solely to keep the mosquito population of the Keys under control. An employee of the Mosquito Control District visits every home in the Keys every three months. While there, the employee looks for potential mosquito breeding areas and gives out any helpful information they can to keep the population under control. There has even been a proposal to release genetically-modified mosquitos to counter the mosquito-borne diseases of chikungunya and dengue. Although there are no known locally-contracted cases of the former, the latter has periodically arisen in parts of Key West.

Travel Bit Number 83: No Name Key (Mile 30.2)

No Name Key — named in a manner that makes those of us who have struggled to name a pet or child feel somewhat better — has been so-called since at least the mid-1800s. It is home to many key deer, and for years found itself the southern end of the ferry portion of the Overseas Highway. The remnants of the mooring for the ferry remain in the waters off of the key, and you can see them in satellite images of the island.

Although unconfirmed, No Name Key supposedly played host to the CIA during the Cuban Missile Crisis and the Bay of Pigs Invasion. At the time, No Name Key had no full-time residents and thus made an easily-accessible but private training ground for Cuban revolutionaries. Whether this rumor will ever be confirmed remains to be seen.

More recently, No Name Key was subject to a county ordinance that prohibited it from connecting to the power grid of the Florida Keys. Thus, if a resident of No Name Key wanted electricity, it had to come from a natural source, such as solar or wind power, or a generator. While most people would not want to live without electricity (and air conditioning), the ordinance likely kept the population from growing much despite the island being accessible by car.

Today, No Name Key has fewer than fifty homes. In 2013, the county repealed the ordinance preventing residents from connecting to the power grid. Today, much of No Name Key is linked to the power grid. Whether this will result in more growth on the island or if it will mostly keep its remote nature remains to be seen.

Travel Bit Number 84: Landsharks

Today, sharks in the Keys are a tourist attraction: their dark shapes can be seen slowly swimming beneath the bridges of the Overseas Highway, and SCUBA divers and snorkelers regularly encounter them on dives on the reefs and shipwrecks of the islands. In the 1920s, though, sharks became a big business in the Florida Keys when a shark oil plant opened on Big Pine Key.

Shark oil has long been a folk remedy. Today, people use it as a treatment for maladies ranging from small cuts to HIV. Hydenoil Products opened in 1923 on Big Pine Key as a plant that processed shark liver oil into a supposed remedy for many ailments. Unlike many fish, which stay buoyant thanks to a swim bladder, a shark regulates its buoyancy through its liver. Because of this, shark livers are extremely large. Up to 75 percent of a shark's liver consists of oil that can be used in shark liver oil remedies. In some sharks, the liver can be 20 percent of a shark's overall weight.

After a few years in business, the shark oil plant employed 25 men and caught and processed over 100 sharks a day. A shark oil plant wasted virtually no part of the shark. Their skins were shipped north for conversion into shagreen, a tough leather. Their fins went to Asia for use in soup, and their heads became glue. Their pancreases made life-saving insulin, and their vertebrae became walking canes. Other parts of the sharks were sold as curios or made into fertilizer.

With so many sharks coming through the plant, it was almost inevitable that workers would find interesting items in the stomachs of the sharks. The most interesting (or macabre) of these finds was the human arm and head found in one shark's stomach. Police traced the body parts to the victim of a plane crash near Havana, only somewhat to the relief of vacationers in the Keys.

After only eight years, the plant closed in 1931 as it was unable to pay the salaries of the men it employed, despite its seemingly brisk business.

Travel Bit Number 85: Snakes on a Key (Mile 27.0)

The Keys are home to numerous types of snakes, four of which are poisonous. Cottonmouths are typically found in the marshes, swamps, and wet areas of the Keys, while Coral Snakes are in the dry pines and hammocks. There are two kinds of rattlesnakes in the Keys as well: the Eastern Diamondback and the Pygmy. The latter of these is the poisonous snake residents and visitors to the Keys are likely to encounter, as it often lives in residential areas.

One of the Keys is more associated with snakes than any other: Ramrod Key. The island gets its name from a ship — the Ramrod — which wrecked on a reef near the island in the early-1800s. More recently, the island has developed a reputation for being home to an unusually large number of rattlesnakes. In the 1960s, the snakes were so abundant that residents would burn off undeveloped lots and shoot the snakes as they fled the flames, hoping to reduce their population.

Although poisonous snakes pose a small danger to visitors, it is two types of non-poisonous, invasive snakes that are most worrisome to the Keys: the boa and the python. Both boas and pythons have become breeding residents of the Everglades. As good swimmers, there is a worry that they will find their way to the Keys and displace native species. On Key Largo, the major concern is that the snakes will arrive and wipe out the fragile populations of two endangered species, the Key Largo woodrat and the Key Largo cotton mouse. There are already efforts underway to keep the invasive snakes out of the Keys, including trapping programs on Key Largo, that will hopefully prove successful.

Travel Bit Number 86: Alligators and Crocodiles in the Keys

The Florida Keys are home to both American alligators (*Alligator mississippiensis*) and American crocodiles (*Crocodylus acutus*). The latter are more plentiful in the Keys, and people regularly see them in the Upper and Middle Keys. They even make occasional trips to the Lower Keys. In 2003, a crocodile showed up at Dry Tortuga National Park, about 70 miles (110 km) beyond the end of the road in Key West. Park officials named him Cletus, and he became a popular feature at the park. In 2017, after becoming something of a pest — he was frequenting the swimming beach at the park — park officials captured Cletus and moved him to Everglades National Park.

Alligators in the Keys are rarer than crocodiles. The best place to see an alligator is likely at the Blue Hole. (Travel Bit Number 81.) A study in the early 1980s found approximately 130 alligators spread throughout the Keys, but over 50 of these were hatchlings and juveniles.

As a general rule, crocodiles are more dangerous than their alligator cousins. Although alligators regularly attack people in Florida, this is a function of alligators greatly outnumbering crocodiles. Crocodiles are typically more prone to attack humans than their slower and more docile alligator cousins. While alligators regularly injure people in Florida, the only known crocodile attack in the state occurred in the Florida Keys in April 2011. A couple kayaking home around 3:30 AM flipped their kayak. While in the water, a crocodile bit each of them on the leg and gave them a story to be told for the rest of their lives.

Florida Fish & Wildlife Conservation Commission – American Alligator:
  myfwc.com/wildlifehabitats/profiles/
  reptiles-and-amphibians/reptiles/alligator

Florida Fish & Wildlife Conservation Commission – American Crocodile:
  myfwc.com/wildlifehabitats/wildlife/american-crocodile/

Travel Bit Number 87: The Mon-Keys

Sometime around 1972, two Keys, Key Lois (formerly Loggerhead Key) and Raccoon Key, became home to some of the more unexpected residents of the Florida Keys: a large group of rhesus monkeys. Rhesus monkeys have been used extensively for research and drug testing. They have been sent to space and were the first cloned primate. They even gave their name to the positive and negative rhesus blood factor.

Like many rhesus monkeys before them, those living on Key Lois and Raccoon Key were research monkeys. The islands proved an ideal home in many ways for the monkeys. Their owners left them on the two islands to fend for themselves, and by all accounts, they flourished. With only a daily supply run of food and fresh water brought in (as well as periodic cleanings of the islands to collect the feces that would otherwise overwhelm them), the monkeys grew from a population of 100 to thousands without any further human intervention. The population was so healthy that every year, over 1,000 monkeys were being taken off the island for research use. The going rate for a monkey from the islands — known to researchers as the biggest and healthiest rhesus monkeys in the world — was from $1,500 to $4,500.

Although the monkeys thrived on the islands, people could see their effect on the two Keys from the sky. Key Lois has a tidal river that runs through its center, separating it into what looks like two islands from above. On one side of the tidal river, the island appeared to be a lush, green paradise, while the other side appeared a shade of grey. The grey side was that upon which the monkeys lived. The monkeys' climbing, scratching, and eating denuded their side of all vegetation and exposed the limestone through soil erosion. This destruction of the islands led to the removal of the monkeys from the islands in 1999 in an effort to stop water pollution near the Keys and prevent further damage.

Travel Bit Number 88: Sponges

Until the mid-1800s, most of the sponges used in the United States came from the Mediterranean. Sponges were used for cleaning, as padding, and even as municipal water filters from at least the days of the ancient Greeks. Traditionally, free divers harvested sponges. The divers would spot a sponge on the ocean floor and swim to retrieve it without the use of any source of air beyond their lungs. In the mid-1800s, soft sponges were discovered in the Florida Keys and the Bahamas, and the United States found itself with a sponge source much closer to home.

Sponges are a living creature which can be "farmed." You can cut a sponge into pieces, and each piece will grow into a large sponge within two to four years. This reproductive aspect of the sponge is what allowed the sponge industry to thrive in the same parts of Greece for centuries. The divers pulled the sponge away from the rocks on which they grew, but as they did, a piece of the sponge remained behind. In a few years, they could return to the spot, and a sponge would have grown from the small portion that remained behind.

As the 1800s ended, the Key West sponge industry had grown to a $750,000 per year industry, or $20 million in today's dollars. The industry flourished thanks to an inability at the time to make artificial sponges. Methods of harvesting at that time, however, pulled the sponge entirely from the rocks on which they lived. This method prevented the sponges from re-growing, as they had for centuries in the Mediterranean. Thus, the sponges in the Keys became harder to find and harvest. Up the west coast of Florida, a burgeoning Greek community in Tarpon Springs started harvesting their deep waters using sustainable techniques, and the industry shifted up the coast, where it remains today.

Travel Bit Number 89: Cudjoe Key (Mile 21.0)

We have lost the history of Cudjoe Key's original settlement, but many strongly suspect that the island was founded or settled by runaway slaves. All ex-slaves that settled in the Keys were considered free men, no matter the circumstances that brought them to the Keys. There is only one known slaveholder known to have made the Keys home; that was Jacob Housman, of Indian Key. (Travel Bit Number 44.) Thanks to this policy, the Keys were a destination for many escaped or runaway slaves.

The suspected origin of Cudjoe Key's name arises out of this history. Cudjoe (or a variation thereof) was a common slave name. Some African communities and cultures traditionally name their children after the day of the week on which a child is born. As an example, in some parts of Africa a boy born on Wednesday would be given the name "Kweku," and a boy born on Friday would be named "Kofi." Several African cultures give the name "Cudjoe" to boys born on Monday. Thus, the name of the Key is suspected to have come from one of its early residents, who was likely a former slave seeking refuge in a place where he could live his life as a free man.

Travel Bit Number 90: Blimp Road (Mile 21.0)

Visitors passing Blimp Road in the past often kept an eye on the sky: Blimp Road was once home to "Fat Albert," a large, white surveillance blimp that made the Keys its home for many years. The surveillance Fat Albert conducted was aimed at keeping an ear on Cuba, as well as the drug smugglers whose boats ply the waters off the Keys and southern Florida. At 175 feet (53 m) long and 58 feet (17.7 m) across, Fat Albert was a significant presence in the sky. Fat Albert was not the only blimp of his kind; they have been or continue to be stationed in several locations, usually on a border or near water.

During his years in the Keys, Fat Albert had numerous mishaps. In 2001, a small plane crashed into the large tether that kept Fat Albert tied to the ground and killed three people. From 1993-1994, three different blimps were lost to high winds. In 1991, Fat Albert broke free of his tether and floated over the Everglades. When he finally came down, the location was so remote it took a week to recover the blimp—and even then, it required helicopters to get him out. In 1984, Fat Albert supposedly had to be shot out of the sky using an air-to-air missile when he floated too close to Cuba after breaking free of his tether.

Travel Bit Number 91: The Bahamas Come to the Keys

Although known for their proximity to Cuba, the Keys have closer cultural ties to the Bahamas than Cuba. During the American Revolution, many Tories fled to Florida or the Bahamas, both of which were then-British colonies. In the 1800s, with the rise of wrecking, many residents of the Bahamas — some descended from the very Tories who fled the United States during the Revolution — regularly came to the Keys to work the wrecks. (Travel Bit Number 25).

When wrecking became legitimized, the Bahamians living in the Keys were forced to decide whether to become Americans. Many chose to do so and became some of the original settlers of the Florida Keys. (Travel Bit Number 58.) Their ancestors still live in the Keys today.

Travel Bit Number 92: Bat Tower (Mile 17.0)

Although Mother Nature has blessed the Florida Keys with some of the best weather in the United States, she has cursed them with some of the worst mosquitos. For the entirety of the time people have lived in the Keys, they have sought ways to escape the omnipresent insects. The Bat Tower, a 30 foot (9 m) tall wooden structure on Lower Sugarloaf Key, was one attempt to reduce the mosquito problem.

Richter Clyde Perky, a fishing lodge owner, built the Bat Tower in 1929. He presumed that the bats who would make the Tower home would eat mosquitos and help reduce the mosquito population that plagued the Lower Keys. Unfortunately, upon the construction of the Bat Tower, no bats showed up.

Perky did have a Plan B, though: he would order bats and place them in the Bat Tower. Unfortunately for Perky, Plan B did not go as planned, either. Instead of staying near the Bat Tower, the introduced bats promptly flew away from the Bat Tower, never to return.

The Bat Tower of the Florida Keys was not the only such tower in the country. At some point, there were 14 known bat towers. Prior to 2017, three bat towers remained: the Florida Keys Bat Tower and two in Texas. A fourth tower, located in Florida, is being reconstructed after it burned down several decades ago. Of these towers, only one has been known to actually have been used by bats.

Unfortunately, only two bat towers exist today. Hurricane Irma toppled the Florida Keys Bat Tower. Although it is on the National Registry of Historic Places, it is unknown whether the tower will be rebuilt.

Travel Bit Number 93: Not Your Father's Bunny

On Boca Chica, Saddlebunch, Lower Sugarloaf, and Big Pine Key, as well as several smaller nearby islands, lives the Lower Keys marsh rabbit. A small- to medium-sized rabbit, the Lower Keys marsh rabbit is the smallest of three marsh rabbit species and has short, dark brown fur and a grayish-white belly. The Lower Keys marsh rabbit has a minimal home range, at somewhere between 630 and 780 acres (90-315 ha). It was recognized as an endangered species in 1990. A census is 1999 showed that there were somewhere between 100 and 300 Lower Keys marsh rabbits remaining. The endangered rabbits are threatened by traffic, habitat alteration, exotic vegetation, and stray cats.

Although it looks much like other rabbits found in the Keys and on the mainland, the Lower Keys marsh rabbit does have one trait which sets it apart from other rabbits. In the 1980s, Playboy funded research into the Lower Keys marsh rabbit. In gratitude, the scientific name for the rabbit was designated as *Sylvilagus palustris hefneri* in honor of Playboy's founder, Hugh Hefner. It turns out, Hefner's bunnies are not all of the humankind.

Travel Bit Number 94: Naval Air Station Key West (Mile 8.0)

Boca Chica Key ("Little Mouth Key") is home to Naval Air Station Key West (NAS-Key West), which is a base for training air-to-air combat fighting for the Navy. NAS-Key West supports operational and readiness requirements for the Department of Defense, Department of Homeland Security, the National Guard, federal agencies, and allied forces. Blessed with almost perfect weather, NAS-Key West is within minutes of aerial ranges where training can occur, making it an ideal location for year-round training. Drivers on the Overseas Highway should not be surprised to see more than a few military jets taking off and landing as they drive across Boca Chica Key.

The U.S. military — and in particular, the Navy — has had a long presence in the Florida Keys. On March 25, 1822, Matthew C. Perry planted the U.S. flag on Key West. A year later, the Navy established a base there, near present-day of Mallory Square. This first base existed primarily to stop piracy in and around the Keys. During the Mexican-American War, the Navy expanded the base. Fort Zachary Taylor on Key West dates to this period of expansion. During the Spanish-American War, the last voyage of the U.S.S. Maine began in Key West and ended fatefully in Havana.

The location of what is known today as NAS-Key West on Boca Chica dates to 1917 when the Navy established it as a submarine base during World War I. At the time, the station supplied oil to the U.S. fleet and kept the Germans away from Mexican oil supplies. The role of the station soon expanded because of its almost perfect location for year-round work. The World War I era at the station also saw the Navy's first flight, conducted by a Curtiss N-9 Sea Plane.

Between World War I and World War II, the Navy

decommissioned the station and used only periodically. With the outbreak of World War II, the station became NAS-Key West and served as a base for monitoring and pursuing German U-Boats in the waters around Florida. (Travel Bit Number 49.) The Navy has used the base continuously ever since.

Travel Bit Number 95: Cubans in Jets

Traveling by military jet, it can take less than 15 minutes to get from Cuba to Key West. NAS-Key West is well-aware of this proximity because twice, military jets from Cuba have landed at the airport and deposited their defecting pilots on American shores.

The first time this happened was on March 20, 1991. On that day, Major Orestes Lorenzo Perez, a member of the Cuban Air Force, landed his MIG-23 aircraft at NAS-Key West. Although he radioed his intent to land, Lorenzo Perez circled Key West several times without being picked up by radar before landing. Upon arrival, the base commander greeted Lorenzo Perez with a hearty handshake and a short greeting: "Welcome to the United States."

On September 17, 1993, the scenario repeated itself with another pilot, although this time, the MIG-21 was picked up by radar as it crossed between Cuba and Key West.

The story of Lorenzo Perez, the first of these two defectors, does not end with his landing at NAS-Key West. In December 1992, Lorenzo Perez headed back to Cuba via a Cessna, but not to renege on his defection. Instead, he returned to pick up his wife and two sons, whom he had left behind when making his original flight. After arranging for their pickup by sending a messenger to Cuba via Mexico, Lorenzo Perez wave skipped his plane very low across the Florida Straits to avoid detection, then landed on a Cuban coastal highway. Next to the road, his wife and two sons were awaiting his arrival. After picking them up, the reunited family returned to the United States, all seeking asylum thanks to the bold efforts of Lorenzo Perez. They continue to reside in the United States today.

Travel Bit Number 96: Stock Island (Mile 5.2)

The last island on the Overseas Highway before reaching Key West is Stock Island. Home to many people who work on Key West, Stock Island's name comes from either the name of an early settler on the island or the herds of livestock that the residents of Key West once kept there. It is home to several of Key West's tourist attractions, including the Botanical Garden and the Key West Golf Course, one of only five 18-hole courses in the Florida Keys. The island was previously home to the Islander, a drive-in movie theater that closed in 1984, but which lives on in a line from the Jimmy Buffett song *Grapefruit, Juicy Fruit*: "Drive-In/guzzle gin/commit a little mortal sin/it's good for the soul."

The most prominent feature on Stock Island is not one of these tourist attractions, but a giant hill on the island, rising 90 feet (27 m) above sea level. Though not a natural feature, this is the highest location in the Keys. Commonly referred to as "Mount Trashmore," this giant hill is the former Key West Landfill. Having been replaced in 1987 by an incinerator and trucks to ship other garbage back to the mainland, Mount Trashmore now silently watches over the Key West Golf Course and Stock Island. Recently, Mt. Trashmore has become the site of large-scale public art. After the September 11 terrorist attacks, a U.S. flag was created on its face. A similar rainbow flag was also created one year for Key West's Pride celebration.

Travel Bit Number 97: The Cuban Missile Crisis

On October 15, 1962, a U-2 spy plane traveling over Cuba discovered that the Russians were building missile sites in Cuba. A week later, on October 22, President Kennedy went on national television to announce that the United States would blockade Cuba and demand the disassembly of the sites and the removal of the missiles. For the next six days, the two countries hovered in a state of near-nuclear war. On October 28, the Russians announced that they would dismantle the missile sites, ending the Crisis.

At less than 100 miles (160 km) from Cuba, the Florida Keys were almost inevitably going to be involved in the Cuban Missile Crisis. One would also have thought that the United States would already have defenses in place leading up to the crisis, but on that point, one would be wrong. On October 15, 1962, there were no defenses against Cuba — except the already-existing NAS-Key West — in the Keys. There were not even any missiles in the Keys capable of reaching Cuba.

That would quickly change. By October 28, there was a missile unit on Smathers Beach in Key West. Nearby, tourists gawked and took pictures of the island's latest attraction. Although mobilized, the new missiles were not entirely operational by the end of the crisis. Lesson learned, the Keys would become a major location for defenses against Cuba (and the Russians) shortly after the crisis. One of these sites that came into being was on North Key Largo. In 1979, the sites were closed. Today, little remains of this piece of Florida Keys history. The locations of the radar and missile sites are on state-owned land. All of them have already been dismantled or are likely to be demolished soon. In the meantime, look for them when coming into the Keys via Card Sound Road.

Travel Bit Number 98: Monroe County Sheriff's Office Animal Farm

Stock Island is home to a location where individuals who have too much fun on their Florida Keys vacations end up: the Monroe County Detention Center. The Detention Center is what one would expect of a local jail, with one notable exception: it is home to the only prison-run animal farm in the United States.

The Detention Center was built to withstand a major hurricane. As such, it sits 11 feet (3 m) above the ground, to handle any storm surge and flooding that comes with a large storm. Until 1994, Monroe County used the area beneath the building for parking and inmate evacuation. That year, the Key West Golf Course developed a problem: drivers regularly killed the ducks who made their home at the golf course when they crossed the road. To solve the dead duck problem, the ducks were brought to the Detention Center, where they could be penned in instead of becoming road kill. Someone put in a pond for them and workers at the Detention Center started taking their breaks at nearby picnic tables to enjoy their new web-footed friends. Shortly after that, the Miami SPCA called the Detention Center and inquired as to whether they could house an abandoned blind horse. Inmates constructed a pen for the horse, who became the next resident of the Detention Center.

After that, animals regularly found their way to the Detention Center — many from law enforcement confiscation. Today, the Detention Center has a full-time "farmer" who oversees the maintenance of the Detention Center as well as the animal farm. The farm is now home to a large and eclectic group of animals. Among others, there are sloths, alpacas, miniature horses, parrots, and turkeys. One popular resident is Albert, an African Spurred Tortoise. Albert is so large that he could break down his owner's fence and roam around his Key West neighborhood. His owner donated him to the farm to prevent Albert from his slow terrorizing of the neighbors. There are three other tortoises, two of which were confiscated from a home in Colorado during a drug raid.

The animal farm is maintained by the inmates of the Detention Center, who receive training in working with the animals through their maintenance of the farm. They can apply this knowledge once released. Another benefit of the farm is that inmates get to experience compassion to and from another living creature. Many of the inmates value this compassion more than the training.

Monroe County Sheriff's Office – Animal Farm:
        www.keysso.net/farm

Travel Bit Number 99: The Great Florida Birding Trail

With 500 birding sites and over 2,000 miles (3,200 km) of trails, the Great Florida Birding Trail provides birders and others looking to see birds in their natural habitats a huge number of environments and locations to do so. Ten of those 500 sites are in the Florida Keys, stretching from Key Largo to the Dry Tortugas.

Along the Great Florida Birding Trail in the Keys, people regularly spot rare avian visitors to the United States, thanks to its tropical location. For example, the Dry Tortugas are the only significant site in the United States where Sooty Terns breed. During the breeding season, there are tens of thousands of the birds on Bush Key, each of them loudly proclaiming their right to the particular territory where they are nesting. On Key West, Fort Zachary Taylor is the first dry land many migrating birds see after their long migrations. It has become a frequent site of rare bird sightings, despite being next to one of the main cruise ship docks.

Great Florida Birding Trail Website:
   floridabirdingtrail.com

Travel Bit Number 100: The Dry Tortugas

Beyond Key West and the end of the Overseas Highway lie several more islands in the Florida Keys chain: the Marquesas Keys and the Dry Tortugas. The Marquesas are an uninhabited group of islands about 20 miles (30 km) west of Key West. The Marquesas encircle a lagoon called Mooney Harbor. Today, the islands are part of the Key West National Wildlife Refuge and are well-known for their fishing.

Beyond the Marquesas lie the Dry Tortugas. About 70 miles (110 km) west of Key West, the Dry Tortugas were so named because they had no sources of natural water and the humped shapes of the islands resembled tortoises from a distance. "Tortuga" is the Spanish word for "turtle" or "tortoise." How it came to be that we use one English word and one Spanish word for the name of the Dry Tortugas is a mystery.

The seven islands of the Dry Tortugas, along with the waters surrounding them, form Dry Tortugas National Park. Dry Tortugas National Park is one of the most isolated and well-preserved parks in the National Park System.

The Dry Tortugas are home to Fort Jefferson, a fort on Garden Key which was never fully finished. Begun in 1847, construction on the fort ceased during the Civil War, when the island became a military prison for the United States. The military continued to use the island as a prison until 1874. Among the prison's inmates was Dr. Samuel Mudd. He arrived at Fort Jefferson for his role in fixing John Wilkes Booth's leg after President Lincoln's assassination.

Fort Jefferson never saw an attack during its active period. Despite never being completed, it is still the largest masonry structure in the Western Hemisphere with over 16 million bricks used in its construction.

The waters around the Dry Tortugas have long been

treacherous for ships. The first recorded shipwreck in their waters was in 1622. During hurricanes, entire islands in the Dry Tortugas have simply disappeared. Sometimes, those islands reappear with a different shape and shoreline. Three of the Dry Tortugas disappeared entirely during the 1800s, and another disappeared in 1935. These constantly changing waters are one of the reasons navigation in the waters around the Dry Tortugas has been fraught with danger since the arrival of the Spanish ships long ago.

National Park Service – Dry Tortugas National Park:
        nps.gov/drto/index.htm

Travel Bit Number 101: Key West (Mile 0.0)

The end of the Overseas Highway is also the ultimate destination of many travelers on the road: Key West. One officially arrives on the island of Key West at Mile 4.1; Mile 0 is a few miles later in the Old Town area of the city. The end of the Overseas Highway is near many of the city's tourist attractions, from Ernest Hemingway's home to Duval Street. Then again, being less than four miles long and two miles wide, nothing on the island is truly very far from the tourist attractions.

The name Key West is either a reference to its location as the westernmost island in the Keys with a reliable source of water (as it previously had some shallow pools where water would sit after a storm) or an English transliteration of the Spanish *Cayo Hueso*, meaning "Bone Key." Key West was the first major settlement in the Florida Keys; it is both the name of the island and the city that covers it. Claimed for the United States in 1822, by 1889, the city of Key West was the largest and richest city in not just the Keys but all of Florida.

Today, while it is no longer the largest city in Florida, Key West is a major tourist destination with resorts and regular visits by cruise ships. For anyone looking to learn more about Key West, we recommend picking up a copy of 101 Travel Bits: Key West.

Monroe County Tourist Development Council – Key West:
   www.fla-keys.com/key-west

The Books in the 101 Travel Bits Series

The Alaska Highway

The Florida Keys & Overseas Highway

Gettysburg

The Grand Canyon

Key West

Rocky Mountain National Park

Theodore Roosevelt National Park

Yellowstone National Park

Yosemite National Park

Please see our website at www.101travelbits.com for information on purchasing additional books in the 101 Travel Bits series or click on the above links for ordering information.

Coming Soon

The Everglades

Glacier National Park

Made in the USA
Middletown, DE
24 April 2021

38364469R00095